Developing High Quality Observation, Assessment and Planning in the Early Years

What is meant by high quality observation in the Early Years? How do you devise effective next steps for young children that build on their interests? How do you ensure that you meet the needs of all the children in your care?

Offering a fresh approach, this practical toolkit offers a complete guide to observation, assessment and planning in the Early Years. It clearly explains the principles of good practice in this area and provides training tools to help practitioners develop their knowledge and skills and embed these principles into their setting. The focus throughout is on helping practitioners to create their own systems for observation, planning and assessment that are appropriate for the children they work with.

All the material in the book has been fully tried, tested and proven to work and the methods described can be tailored to meet the needs of individual practitioners. Featuring a wide range of case studies to illustrate how the principles work in practice, the book includes:

- making effective observations and assessments;
- recognising the characteristics of effective learning;
- engaging parents in their children's learning;
- identifying next steps and learning priorities;
- dealing with barriers and maintaining quality over time.

With fully photocopiable resources throughout and downloadable training sessions to accompany the book, this is an essential toolkit for all Early Years managers, leaders and those involved in setting support.

Lisa Sancisi has been an Early Years teacher in primary schools for over 20 years. For the last 6 years she has also worked as a children's centre support teacher as part of Hampshire's Early Years Advisory Team supporting settings and schools, delivering training and profile moderation and supporting family learning in children's centres.

Margaret Edgington is a specialist in work with young children, having worked as an Early Years teacher, educational home visitor, advisory teacher, NNEB tutor and nursery school head teacher. Most recently, she has offered a training, advice and consultancy service across the UK (and sometimes abroad), and written on the subject of early childhood education, including her books *The Foundation Stage Teacher in Action*, 3rd edition, 2004, and *The Great Outdoors,* 2nd edition, 2014. She has worked as a mentor/consultant to a number of nursery and primary schools, day nurseries, pre-schools and children's centres. She is a Vice President of the National Campaign for Real Nursery Education and a founder member of the Open EYE Campaign.

Developing High Quality Observation, Assessment and Planning in the Early Years

Made to measure

Lisa Sancisi and Margaret Edgington

Routledge
Taylor & Francis Group
LONDON AND NEW YORK

First published 2015
by Routledge
2 Park Square, Milton Park, Abingdon, Oxon OX14 4RN

and by Routledge
711 Third Avenue, New York, NY 10017

Routledge is an imprint of the Taylor & Francis Group, an informa business

British Library Cataloguing-in-Publication Data
A catalogue record for this book is available from the British Library

Library of Congress Cataloging in Publication Data
A catalog record for this title has been requested

ISBN: 978-1-138-80803-4 (hbk)
ISBN: 978-1-138-80804-1 (pbk)
ISBN: 978-1-315-75076-7 (ebk)

Typeset in Bembo
by FiSH Books Ltd, Enfield
Printed and bound in Great Britain by Ashford Colour Press Ltd, Gosport, Hampshire

Contents

Acknowledgements

We would like to thank the following contributors for their help, support, enthusiasm and work, which have made this publication possible:

Children and families at Earley St Peter's Primary school
West Green Day Nursery
Farnborough Grange Nursery and Infant school
Sadie Shipley
Carrie Maries
Natalie Laidlaw
Mena Avery
Sara Macdonald
Kate Bradbury
Sue Skerrat
Practitioners from settings and schools in Hart and Rushmoor who participated in the projects
Members of the Early Years Advisory Team that supported the projects and participants

1 Background and rationale

As a local advisory team in Hart and Rushmoor, we regularly review our work with Early Years' settings, to look at how effective the work has been and how we can improve. Throughout our support work, we noted that many settings were requesting support around **planning**. As a result we were replicating the same type of support in lots of different settings. We knew that high quality training had been delivered locally too. However, practitioners found it hard to take messages back from one training session to make a real difference to practice and provision. We had also assessed that although settings had asked for support in developing planning systems, the foundations for this needed to be embedded in the first instance; **through developing robust practice in** *observational assessment*.

A new approach

So the team decided a **new approach** to training was needed. We knew that we wanted every setting to have its own *'OAP' expert* (Observation, Assessment and Planning) who would be well trained and well equipped. This **'OAP champion'** (yes, we did chuckle at the term initially, and no, they didn't need a bus pass!) would need to lead others, share the training and development of skills in order to improve practice. They would need to lead ongoing, long term developments within their setting to ensure robust practice in OAP would be effectively embedded.

In order to support the creation of our 'OAP champions' we needed a **carefully structured development programme**. We wanted to deliver portions of high quality training **interwoven** with a variety of support opportunities. These include setting visits and support surgeries, planned to sit in between each training session. This would be the model for our project approach – a training session, then a support surgery, followed by our support visits, then the next training session.

We hoped to keep the **number of delegates in each session quite low**. This was planned to raise practitioner confidence, which would be key to enable them to lead change. Each practitioner needed to feel confident to discuss barriers or areas they found difficult in order for real developments to be made. The small group size would promote discussion, enable the group to get to know each other, support each other, share ideas and develop an effective working relationship with the trainer. Each setting would be asked to send a **lead practitioner** to the training, someone who would be in a position to effect and manage development and change.

The right trainer

Our next action was to approach a trainer. We knew that **Margaret Edgington** was an expert in the area who had already worked successfully to deliver training to Hampshire Early Years' settings and schools; we hoped she would be able to lead the training element of our project. We needed a confident, **inspirational and experienced trainer** who would be able to work flexibly to directly meet the needs of the participants. She would need to help our delegates find practical solutions to their challenges. She would also need to embrace exploring issues that may arise spontaneously during the sessions. To our delight Margaret was enthusiastic and able to do this for us; and in our discussions with her, the project approach further emerged and strengthened. Margaret was able to bring her experience of training and working with schools and settings to inform our plans for the project. We decided that communication between the team and Margaret would be vital in order to shape the training to fully meet the needs of the delegates. Our session plans would be based on our assessment of the practitioners' needs and the training programme would be **flexible** to accommodate this.

The project was planned as follows; four half-day sessions of training delivered by Margaret, planned over two terms. Between each session the delegates attended support surgeries where they could further discuss issues raised in the training. We ensured that during the support visits we carried out to settings, we always reflected on their OAP project developments. The information from surgeries and visits was shared with Margaret who then adapted her training to explore issues further as necessary. To keep the group size small, we offered two parallel sessions – one morning cohort and one afternoon cohort.

To fully support the implementation of the training within the settings, we decided that *all members of our team should attend the training, to* **support their settings during the sessions.** This would enable us to work with the delegates during the practical parts of the sessions but also served another purpose. We were later able to clarify, reiterate and consolidate training messages through the surgeries we delivered between sessions or one to one during support visits. We had heard the same messages at first hand and this was invaluable for our work.

The project begins

As the project began Margaret agreed that electronic versions of her training slides could be shared with the project delegates so they could use these in their work to support colleagues through training. Delegates used the slides for staff meetings and therefore shared the methods Margaret had used to explore understanding. The sessions were powerful in that they were delivered with a high level of practitioner involvement and discussions; the practical activities offered were then taken back and used in settings. For example, Margaret offered a session exploring '**good observation/bad observation?**' The practitioners looked at examples of short observations and worked together to decide which were useful, which were not. This activity was powerful and repeated in many settings after the training.

The project first ran for the PVI (Private, Voluntary and Independent) sector only. The success of the project then enabled the team to follow this with a project for schools, which would mirror themes and the systematic approaches explored in the first project. Schools and settings would then be able to share evidence of children's learning and achievements with a joint understanding.

A challenge to our 'project approach' was delegate illness, where one session was missed over the course of the training. Any delegates were signposted to attend the *catch-up surgery session* that was delivered by the team. In the case of a new teacher who only attended the last session (in place of her colleague on sick leave), we carried out a support visit before the session to go through the themes using the training slides, notes and suggested forms Margaret had given to delegates to support their practice.

As the PVI project was mirrored in the schools project, slightly different themes emerged and were covered: the revised EYFS (Early Years Foundation Stage), the revised EYFS Profile and engaging parents. The teachers welcomed a session delivered by Margaret for head teachers. This reflected the themes of the training as well as how to support their EYFS teacher, an introduction to the value of play as a vehicle for learning and the importance of child initiated play.

A summary of key points:

- we reflected on our offer in order to develop a new approach;
- an expert in each setting – someone in a lead role;
- development of practitioner confidence;
- good quality trainer, clear training messages;
- a flexible approach – matched to the needs and pace of the learners;
- reflection, revisiting and sharing;
- support and training interwoven;
- peer support;
- practitioner voice to shape the training;
- an interactive and practical approach;
- tools to share practice back at the setting;
- empowering practitioners to lead and innovate.

This publication

This publication has grown out of our project and the vision for it is to support the development of new 'OAP champions'. It partly celebrates the achievements and the commitment of the participants through the case studies, but it also serves to support the continued development of practice in this area.

The publication has, at its heart, the content of each of the four training sessions delivered by Margaret during the project.

The first training session begins in Chapter Two; it is the exploration of observational assessment. What do we mean by 'observation'? Why should we observe? There is a consideration of the types of observation and tasks that enable us to think 'Is this an effective observation?' 'What does this tell us?'

Chapter Three explores 'Next Steps' in learning and development and thoughts on engaging parents. How do we find appropriate and effective next steps in learning for children? What do we need to consider?

Chapter Four considers the stages of planning and moving from observational assessment to planning for learning. The section contains aspects to consider when reflecting on your planning system – 'Is the planning flexible?' 'Do we capture the spontaneous planning that takes place?' 'Are the learning intentions clear?'

Chapter Five is the content of a session focused on 'The Characteristics of Effective Learning'. The three characteristics are included in the training as they are essential for practitioners to consider in their observations, assessments and planning. Practitioners, who may feel accustomed to observing, assessing and planning for areas of learning and development, will be supported to consider the characteristics alongside these. They will be supported to consider *how* children learn, not just *what* they are learning, as they observe, assess and plan for children.

Chapter Six is based on a session for head teachers. It is almost a 'brief tour of' the four training sessions that precede it. It is useful as a 'light touch' guide for other stakeholders such as management teams or committees, to share information on the underlying themes.

Chapter Seven is a compilation of case studies from delegates on the project from a variety of settings, with a range of starting points, all of whom made developments as a result of their project involvement. We are very grateful to them and all the delegates for their participation.

Chapter Eight is simply a rough guide to tracking children's progress, followed by a 'health warning' from Margaret on the dangers of over-reliance on numerical data.

At the end of the publication we have offered some useful sheets for consideration and a Frequently Asked Questions sheet from Margaret.

Another useful addition to this publication is the inclusion of an online resource, courtesy of Margaret. During the project, Margaret very kindly and generously agreed to share this set of PowerPoint slides with the delegates. The delegates worked with these training materials in our sessions with Margaret and then were able to take them back to share practice back in the setting. Many used the PowerPoint slides as presentations in staff meetings to share the training with their peers and to support discussions. The PowerPoint slides that Margaret wrote and then used to deliver the training for us are available for you to download at www.routledge.com/9781138808041

We hope a setting manager or lead practitioner could pick up this publication and follow Margaret's training sessions. They would act as a **step-by-step guide to implementing a robust system** over a period of time. Once systems are established in a setting, it could be used to 'dip into' to review and reflect on practices to maintain the quality of observations and assessments. New members of staff could use this booklet as a toolkit to support their developing practice in a team where the principles are firmly embedded.

This publication can also serve to develop practice in the field of quality improvement, through the exploration of new models of support and training. The case studies are a testament to the impact of this type of project approach, which is flexible and adapts to the need of the participants. The flexibility of the approach allows the delegates to fully participate in their development of practice, to determine the focus and pace of the training; revisiting challenging areas and problem solving as issues emerge. The training develops to meet the needs of the learners as individuals and as a cohort. Through this model we wanted to offer practitioners what we offer our most important partners – *the children*; that is, learning that meets their needs, is meaningful and is **'Made to Measure'**.

Happy reading – and good luck for when you run your own mini 'project'!

The content of the training

The aim of the training was to give the practitioners attending the confidence, knowledge and skills to enable them to take a lead in the development of observation, assessment and planning practice in their setting. The rest of this section includes the main content of each of the four sessions (which was adapted and developed according to the needs of each group) and it is hoped it will help other leaders in settings develop their OAP practice. Although the training had to reflect the English Early Years Foundation Stage Framework, most of the material is relevant to all Early Years practitioners wishing to develop their practice in the area of observation based assessment and planning. By describing the training and some of the issues that arose, and also providing access to the PowerPoint slides used for the sessions, it is hoped that other trainers and setting leaders will be able to run bespoke sessions for other practitioners.

The order of the content was chosen carefully. Many practitioners want to know about planning, but, actually, planning is dependent on effective observation and assessment and it is vital to start by evaluating their quality before thinking about planning.

2 Session 1: Making effective observations and assessments

Practitioners had been asked to bring to the first session:

- 4 or 5 randomly selected short observations (of the kind that that you might write on a Post-it note or sticky label) preferably made by different people in your group/class, and also
- one longer (5 minute) observation of a child engaged in child-initiated play.

This session started with some general points about the complexity involved in assessing young children. The EYFS 2012 emphasises the Unique Child and any approach to assessment must seek to find out about what makes each child unique. Children develop very rapidly in their first five years and it is difficult to be sure we have an accurate view of them at any given moment, as they often surprise us. The reliability of any assessment we make is therefore dependent on:

- **Relationships** – the child needs to trust us and the setting in order to show their full capabilities. This takes some children a long time, particularly children who are learning English as an additional language, who often have a long silent period when they start in a new setting. Children relate differently to different team members and usually show more sophisticated learning to those adults they trust most (think about the child undergoing a developmental test at the doctor's and refusing to co-operate, even though the parent knows the child is perfectly capable of doing what is being asked). It is very important that during the child's settling in period the key person makes a point of developing a trusting relationship with the child and his/her parents. To be fair to children, and to be sure that assessments are reliable, time needs to be taken to get to know the children, and to help them feel secure and confident in the setting. Children learning English as an additional language may have a lengthy silent period and will trust more quickly if there is someone in the setting that speaks their language, and if the resources reflect their cultural and linguistic experience. Assessments carried out too early will be unreliable and therefore meaningless.
- **Environment and context** – children can show some attitudes, skills and understanding in one environment or context but not necessarily in another. This is why it is essential to talk to the people who knew the child in their previous setting where they were most confident. Children often surprise, delight and challenge us when they are engaged in self-initiated play activities, where they are in control of their own learning – they are usually less motivated, and less capable of showing what they can do, in adult-directed situations, or if they think they are being tested.
- **Being based on factual, un-biased observations** – observation is the only way we can really tune into each **unique** child.

It is important to remember that each child's development follows a unique pathway and is not linear.

Observation is essential because it helps us to:

- Focus on children as individuals, identifying their starting points (what they can do), strengths, interests, schema (repeated patterns of behaviour such as transporting or positioning) and learning styles, as well as their development and learning. It is particularly important in highlighting children who might otherwise be overlooked (a useful exercise is to ask all team members to make a list, from memory, of the children in the group or setting and then to compare lists – it is often the case that the same children are near the top of everyone's list and similar children at the bottom or, worse, not on the list at all!).
- See each child's personal experience of the setting (the received experience as opposed to the offered experience). It is essential that practitioners look at the setting from each child's perspective and work hard to ensure that all children can find things in the setting that connect with their interests and life experience.
- Raise questions about children's experience and learning, the quality of provision and of adult interactions (thereby challenging assumptions) – observation should be used to help us improve the environment and our interactions with the children. For example, if a child walks away when we speak to them, we need to reflect on what it was about our interaction that was inappropriate.
- Share factual information with colleagues and parents – parents enjoy hearing about the things their child did and said and it is much less threatening to share facts about what the child did, than to share a judgement on his or her behaviour.
- Plan relevant, motivating developmentally appropriate experiences for each child.

What do we mean by observation and what kinds of observations do we need to make?

When we observe, we watch carefully and listen carefully and capture **the facts** of what we see the child do and what we hear the child say. We may capture the facts in our minds, on paper (a quick jotting or a longer narrative piece), in an annotated photo or by collecting and annotating the child's mark-making. Video and audio materials provide another way of capturing facts.

There are 3 main types of observation:

Informal noticing/spontaneous observation

This means having eyes and ears everywhere, noticing what needs to be noticed and often acting on this immediately. In Early Years' work, we often:

- observe what the children are doing;
- assess their needs and interests;
- plan spontaneously how we could address their needs or extend their interests; and
- act on this plan in the space of a few minutes or within the same day.

For example, children playing out of doors were observed taking an interest in some ants. The adult recognised that she could develop this interest and encourage the children to look more closely and use reference books. She suggested the children could use the magnifiers to see the ants more clearly, and get some books to find out more about them and the children responded to these suggestions. Recording of this type of planning has to be done retrospectively and is now often called Spontaneous Planning.

Participant observation

This means observing while working with the children and **briefly** noting **significant responses or development** demonstrated by a child during adult-initiated experiences, and during sessions where you have joined in with child-initiated play – something you haven't seen that child do before or something interesting they have said. What is significant for one child won't necessarily be significant for another. Many practitioners record these quick notes on sticky labels, Post-it notes or pre-printed pro formas. A skill that many practitioners have to learn is keeping their quick jottings brief and making sure they are capturing significant development and learning. We need to avoid writing for writing's sake and taking photos, or keeping pieces of mark-making, without thinking about why this photo is significant.

Focused observation

This means stepping back for about 5 minutes and recording factually as much as possible of what you see and hear happening, and you should record as much as possible of what you see the child doing and hear them saying. The observer is not involved and children should usually be initiating their own learning. This is because child-initiated play shows the child as s/he really is and helps adults tune into the unique child. Many teams now focus on a number of children (2 or 3) each week so that all children are looked at closely. Ideally several members of the team (not just the key person) should observe the same children, so that different perspectives are involved. At the end of the week the practitioners discuss what they have found out about the children they have focused on and identify their learning priorities for the next few weeks.

The focus of all observations is the child. It is not usually helpful to set out with a closed agenda (e.g. to look for a particular skill), as this can prevent us from seeing more important learning for the child and can lead to a tick-list approach, which shows little respect for the unique child.

The next 2 sheets could be used or adapted to use for making focused observations. The first sheet could be used by English practitioners and the second sheet could be used by practitioners working outside of England.

All observational evidence should be:

- factual – should capture what the child does (not what he or she doesn't do, or the adult's interpretation);
- dated – so that progress can be seen over time;
- include the child's and the observer's names;
- contextualised – show the learning context in which the action was taking place;
- include the actual language the child used (not an adult interpretation).

Sheet for recording focused observations

Name: Social context (who the child is with):

Date & time: Learning context (where the child is, indoors or outside):

Age (yrs mths):   Staff member:

Observation:

Assessment (evidence of significant learning):

PSED   L
CL   UW
PD   CD
                                               EAD

Evidence of characteristics of effective learning:

P&E   AL   C&TC

What next? (questions raised, ideas for planning – if appropriate):

Name:

Social context

Date & time:

Learning con
indoors or o

Age (yrs mths):

Staff member:

Observation:

Assessment (what does this observation tell me about the child's interests and capabilities?):

What next? (questions raised, ideas for planning – if appropriate):

actual observations

ck jottings below are typical of ones seen in practitioners' records.

> **Chloe B.**
>
> Chloe shared well when playing with the train set with Olivia.

> **Daniel**
>
> Daniel played in the sand alongside Evie. He enjoyed pouring sand into the sand wheel. No language.

> **Jake**
>
> Jake used a decorator's brush and bucket of water to make marks on the paving slabs.

None of them is useful as they contain judgements or insufficient factual evidence. The first includes the words 'shared well', which is the language of judgement/assessment not observation. The second includes the word 'enjoyed' without any evidence to say why the child appeared to be enjoying himself. It also uses the phrase 'no language'. Observation should capture what the child is doing, not what he is not doing. It is often appropriate for children to play silently. The third example is factual, but not useful because it is not clear what was significant – was it the first time the child had got involved in something? What kind of marks were they? The following two observational jottings are excellent because they are factual and tell us exactly what the child said and did. In the second, we learn why this observation was so significant for Amir. To complete them, they need to be dated, include the practitioner's initials and have a reference to the main area of learning that is demonstrated.

> Billie looked at the Gingerbread man book and said: 'He's gonna catch him isn't he? Then he's gonna eat him.'

> **Amir**
>
> Alone in the home corner.
> Took a pan to the cooker and selected a spoon from the cutlery tray. Said to me, 'Me make soup.' (First time he spoke in English to an adult – children had made soup the previous day.)

All practitioners need to be supported to look at their observations and check they are factual and useful. If when you read one, you are tempted to say 'so what' it's probably not a very useful observation! Photos and examples of mark-making should be accompanied by a note explaining what the child did and said. All observations, photos and pieces of mark-making should show progress in the child's development and learning.

Setting-based follow-up work

During the training we practised making focused observations from DVD material. It is useful to take some video material of a child in your setting engaging in child-initiated play and then ask all staff to make an observation from the clip. If you then compare how each person recorded this observation and analysed it, it is possible to learn a great deal about individual and team strengths and areas for development. Many practitioners, who attended the training, commented that they became much more aware of what they were writing and were able to challenge themselves and others after looking at examples like the ones above.

After the first session of the project participants were asked to give feedback to their colleagues and work together to monitor the quality of observations in their setting – many leaders held a training session based on the training and encouraged staff to look at their learning journals and identify effective and ineffective observations. They were also asked to practise making a focused observation.

Making assessments

An assessment is a judgement about the child's development and learning. Assessment involves reflecting on one or more factual observations and then analysing, interpreting and making judgements about any significant interests, strengths and capabilities the child has demonstrated. Assessments should always be written in positive language. Since the EYFS was introduced in England, many practitioners have tried to match every quick observational jotting or longer observation to statements in the non-statutory Development Matters Guidance (the similarly non-statutory, Early Learning Outcomes document was made available in 2013). In some cases they were advised to do this by advisers. It was never the intention that these documents should be used in this way and trying to do so takes practitioners' attention away from the unique child. When analysing a single observation it is more useful to write a statement of assessment that is relevant to that child rather than copying a statement from a book or list such as *Development Matters* e.g. 'Chloe is now able to use scissors to cut round a square shaped picture in a catalogue' rather than 'Uses one handed tools and equipment'. Sometimes, it is not possible to make an assessment based on a single observation (some simply raise questions that we have to address through further observation or discussion with parents/carers).

Since 2012, it has been suggested that *Development Matters* can be used for summative assessment (when practitioner's carry out progress reviews) – i.e. for practitioners to identify the band that is a 'best fit' for the child's current stage of development and learning. It was also made clear that it is not necessary for a child to have achieved every point in a band. In December 2013 OFSTED published *Subsidiary Guidance; Supporting the Inspection of Maintained Schools and Academies* which stated:

The DfE has placed on its website a new document called 'Early Years Outcomes' as a non-statutory aid to support practitioners. It can be used by childminders, nurseries and others, such as Ofsted inspectors, as a guide to making best-fit judgements about whether a child is showing typical development for their age, may be at risk of delay or is ahead for their age.

There are no national data for attainment on entry to nursery and reception and no prescribed methods of assessing children when they start school. The age bands describe the 'typical development' for children at that age but schools do not have to use these and may have other ways of assessing children when they start school. Inspectors should not use the terms 'average' and 'standards' as there is no 'national average' and there are no standardised expectations for three- and four-year-olds on entry to nursery and reception. Inspectors should discuss with the school's leaders **how** they measure

> children's starting points and the proportions of children that demonstrate development that is typical for their age.
>
> p. 8

This guidance has since been withdrawn and replaced by the *Framework for School Inspection*, July 2014, and the *School Inspection Handbook*, September 2014. In OFTED's *Conducting Early Years Inspections from September 2014* (which covers the private, voluntary and independent sector) it asks inspectors to use the evidence to:

> evaluate how well the provider and practitioners know about, and understand, the progress children are making towards the early learning goals.

and adds in a footnote:

> Inspectors may find it helpful to refer to Early years outcomes, DfE, 2013: a non-statutory guide for practitioners and inspectors to help inform understanding of child development through the early years.
>
> p. 10

Practitioners on the project recognised that many of the colleagues they worked with had had limited training on child development. They found it useful also to purchase and refer to texts written by experts in child development such as those by Jennie Lindon, Carolyn Meggitt and Mary Sheridan et al. (see below for further details).

A number of leaders commented that these specialist child development texts were particularly useful when carrying out the 2-year-old Progress Check.

What assessments do practitioners need to make?

Practitioners need to assess children's:

- interests/motivation (including schema);
- dispositions (how they approach learning. How they are demonstrating the EYFS characteristics of effective learning);
- feelings – how they feel about themselves and about being in the setting;
- preferred learning style;
- relationships and social interaction;
- knowledge and understanding;
- skills;
- access to areas of learning and development – are they accessing all areas over time;
- progress.

They also need to use observation to assess:

- the quality/suitability of the provision and experiences for each child including the use of space;
- the suitability of the daily routine – how well it encourages deep involvement indoors and outside;
- the amount, and quality, of adult interaction.

Making assessments – practical task

Practitioners were asked to read the observation below and make some assessments of child G's development and learning based on the information it contains. The questions underneath the observation were used to focus the practitioners on what evidence they should look for. It was suggested that this activity could be carried out by teams with any focused observation of a child in their setting and could be used to help achieve consistency in the judgements made about individual children.

> G. enters the nursery, selects her name card and sticks it on the board to self-register, says 'bye' to her mum and goes straight across to the cupboard where games are stored. She selects the texture dominoes and puts them on the floor. She places 2 chairs facing each other near the dominoes. She then goes to the creative area and chooses a thin brush from a pot of assorted brushes. She returns to the dominoes and calls to J. 'let's do face painting, what d'you want on your face.' J. replies 'tiger', sits on chair and G. selects a rusty coloured shape on a domino and pretends to paint J.'s face. G. then says 'your turn now, I want to be a clown' and gives J. the brush. They continue taking turns in play for 15 minutes.

Consider the factual focused observation above (or one you have made) and discuss it with your colleagues.

What does this observation tell you about:

- how the child demonstrates the characteristics of effective learning (Playing and Exploring, Active Learning and Creating and Thinking Critically);
- the child's learning and development (have all 7 areas of learning and development in mind as you think about this);
- the quality of the provision and prior teaching.

The session ended with a discussion of the follow-up work to be carried out between sessions. Participants were asked to:

- Share what you have learnt with colleagues in your room/setting and make sure that all observations and assessments made by you and others over the next few weeks are effective. Ask your support teacher to help you with monitoring this.
- A week or so before the next session make at least 1 focused observation of 2 children in your group. Do not analyse these or plan from them – bring them and some recent quick jottings of the same 2 children to the session and we will discuss them then.

Jane, 4 years 8 months

What I saw...

Jane and her friends use blocks, crates, cones and cushions to make a house outdoors. Jane says that they need a front door and they need a number on the house because they live at number 28. She goes to get tape, paper and pens from the creative workshop nearby.

Jane chooses paper to cover the crates they have used to make the front door. Jane puts the paper on top of the crates and she holds a felt tip pen in her fingers. She holds the paper with one hand and begins to write with the other hand. She writes on her house numbers and draws a key hole.

Jane puts down the paper and picks up masking tape. Using her fingernails, Jane picks at the end of the tape. After three or four attempts, the end comes up and Jane pulls the tape. Jane then uses two hands to twist the tape and the tape breaks, leaving a short piece of tape stuck to her finger. Jane attaches the tape to the top of the paper and sticks it on the crates.

She adds another piece and as the paper blows forward at the bottom, Jane looks down at it. She then tears off several pieces of tape to attach the paper to crates at the bottom.

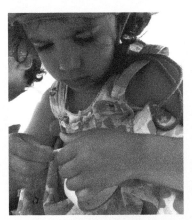

Others begin to join Jane and sit with her. They start to mark-make on the paper as she finishes sticking the paper down with the tape.

She finishes her door, returns to the house and goes to bed.

Jane asks if R would like some help. She tears off pieces of tape for him and shows him how to join his telescope together.

What it tells me...

- The series of photos capture an observation of Jane at work engaged in child-initiated experiences. The observation reveals that Jane has her own ideas and plans that she is able to carry out to completion with success and skill. It reveals that Jane can decide what she needs for a task and knows where to find everything she wants. She seems organised and gathers everything she needs for her plan.
- Jane is quite content for the others to use her work for their own purposes and tells them what she has done. She is open to their ideas and is happy for them to contribute.
- Even though this hasn't been discussed with peers or adults, her idea of using paper will enable her to write on the crate to decorate their front door with numbers and anything else she decides to add. She has shown creativity and imagination in deciding on this way of making a door.
- Jane leans on the crates to write on the house number – this allows Jane to immediately carry out and satisfy her plan to write house numbers. Other observations and interactions with Jane have told me she is interested in numbers and number operations; she can work at a high level in this area. Experience has shown Jane that it might be easier to write on the paper now whilst the paper is flat on the crate rather than after she has put the paper on to the crate in an upright position.
- She uses her knowledge of the world around her to formulate her plans and ideas – for example, 'a front door is important for me in my house, so I'm going to make one and I want to put on the house numbers and key hole. These are important for a front door.'
- Jane is able to persevere even when peeling the tape from the reel is such hard work and could be frustrating. She spends a long time engaged in trying to peel off and then tear the tape. She solves the problem of the wind blowing the paper on the crates by adding tape very securely in all the appropriate areas.
- Also, Jane is happy for others to write on her front door even whilst she is attaching it. She does not have a strong desire to 'keep the door for herself' and can accept that other, less experienced, peers could make their marks on the paper that may not be as skilled as her own. This shows her ability to work very successfully alongside and co-operatively with peers. She is happy to share her work freely with them.
- She is able to decide on a number to go on the house and can write the corresponding numerals very easily.
- Jane is also able to sustain the thread of the role play narrative with her peers, as she is able to return her attention and focus to continue the role play scenario after making the front door.
- Later on in the week, Jane notices a peer struggling with tape; she immediately offers to help him. She tears pieces off for him and helps him join his telescope as she has practised skills in this area.

Hettie, 4 years 1 month

What I saw...

Hettie is engaged in play in the mud kitchen. She is mixing water that she carries from the water butt to the soil in the digging area. She digs up soil from the ground and puts in to the bucket and then says, 'Wait... look there's a worm!' 'Stop!' 'Look, a wormey, let me get him.' She crouches down.

Hettie uses her thumb and index finger to pick up the worm out of the soil in her bucket. She puts it on her hand, and shows her friend, then picks up the worm again to show her friend, the other hand held underneath. She places the worm back on her hand. She looks closely at the worm then runs to show Henry. 'Look what I found. I found a worm.' Henry looks at the worm and smiles at her.

Hettie runs to the teacher. She asks the teacher to take a photo of the worm for her to show her mum later. When asked what she is going to do with the worm she responds, 'I'm going to show George because he lost his worm. I'll put it safe so we don't dig it.' She runs over to George.

What it tells me...

This short observation reveals more about Hettie as a 'learner'. She is able to look carefully, to closely observe details, and spot the worm amongst the mud and water. She wants to share her experience with others and is enthusiastic and excited – she takes pleasure in her achievement of finding and rescuing the worm. In fact as soon as she finds the worm, she is seeking to share the experience with particular peers. She is active, motivated and knows what she plans to do next. Hettie has shown she has knowledge and attitudes that relate to caring for living things and the world around; she reveals that she knows the possible consequences of leaving the worm in the digging area. Hettie also reveals that she has made a link to a previous experience she had with her friend George who lost his worm. It suggests that sharing this 'find' with him and involving him might 'make up' for when he lost his worm – she remembers his feelings and sadness. As she actually handles the worm, she shows care and concern as she is gentle in her handling and as she holds the worm up to show a friend she holds her hand beneath in case it falls. This also reveals that Hettie knows that she can use technology (a photo) to share her experience with her mother in her mother's absence.

Qasim, 3 years 10 months

What I saw...

Qasim sees the sand left at the edge of the sand pit (as a peer digs a hole). Qasim scrapes the sand together into a pile and moulds and pats down the sand. He creates a 'mountain' shape. He spends some time patting this, and scraping and moulding the sand to the 'mountain' shape. This stops as he is asked to tidy up to go home.

The following day. Qasim creates three different sized piles of sand using buckets to transport sand to the area he is working in. He shapes each one with his hands and fingers. He uses his hands to push down on to and to shape the sand and says his fingers make patterns on the sand. He starts to make hand/finger patterns all around the outsides of 'mountain' shapes.

Qasim creates extra height to one of the mounds as he adds additional handfuls of sand to the top. He then goes to the next highest mound and adds to that and then the smallest. He goes back to each one to shape, mould and smooth again.

Others come over and look at his 'work' and Qasim says he is building and he tells them and shows them what he is doing – adding sand to the 'mountains' as he talks.

Qasim sees a small hole in the side of the mountain and he puts his finger in it. He makes another hole in the mountain with his finger and repeats. The side of the mountain cracks when he puts in his finger again and again. He smoothes the cracks and the cracks can no longer be seen.

The next day Qasim works with a friend to create a bigger mountain and quickly explores making holes in the mountain with his finger once again.

What it tells me...

- These observations tell us that Qasim is able to focus and persevere at tasks. He makes a plan and then can carry it out to completion. Qasim experiments with making holes with his finger in the sides of the mountains; he finds it interesting and repeats to see what happens if he carries on. He can plan and carry out those plans, adapt and change and he takes pride in his work.

- He is more than happy to explain what he is doing – it looks like he enjoys being the expert! He is articulate for his age/stage of development and explains processes and ideas to others. He can demonstrate and model to others and tells them his ideas and things he has found out along the way. He looks closely and investigates what he has found and then has ideas about what to do next. He can adapt and change as he creates and has a clear idea of how he wants his work to look. He can set out to do a task and accomplish it without distractions – he can give attention to his work, move attention to a question for a peer, then move back to his work and continue. He can work in collaboration successfully with peers, sharing ideas but also accepting the ideas of others. Qasim shows clear pleasure and satisfaction in his achievements; he is keen to share his work with peers and adults and can recount the processes involved at length – he enjoys talking to adults in particular and often talks at length about what he has done or about what he might do.

- Other assessments have revealed that next steps should include refining and strengthening fine motor control and so this observation can inform the planning for Qasim. The practitioner could intervene **immediately** (a spontaneous plan) to offer a variety of tools to strengthen grip and refine control as Qasim is building the mountains, possibly modelling their use as the adult plays alongside. Alternatively, the adult may use this observed interest in sand construction and mountains to plan for the future; ensuring opportunities for refining and strengthening his fine motor control are supported by a similar experience. This would clearly link his next steps to his interests.

Bibliography

DFE, *Early Years Foundation Stage Statutory Framework* (EYFS), 2012, DFE.

DFE, *Early Years Outcomes*, 2013, available from www.gov.uk/government/publications/early-years-outcomes.

Early Education, *Development Matters*, 2012, Early Education.

Language and Identity in EY Multicultural Settings (Online) Ethnographic Case Studies of an Early Years Centre and Reception Classes Occasional Paper 26 2011, available from www.naldic.org.uk/eal-publications-resources/Shop/shop-products/op26o.

Lindon, J., *Understanding Child Development: 0–8 Years: Linking Theory and Practice*, 2012, Hodder Education.

Meggitt, C., *Child Development: An Illustrated Guide*, 2012, Heinemann.

OFSTED, *Conducting Early Years Inspections from September 2014*, 2014, OFSTED.

Primary Strategy, *Supporting Children Learning English as an Additional Language*, 2007, Department for Children Schools and Families.

Sheridan, M., Sharma, A. and Cockerill, H., *From Birth to Five Years: Children's Developmental Progress*, 4th edition, 2014, Routledge.

Supporting Bilingual Children in the Early Years, available from www.naldic.org.uk/eal-teaching-and-learning/outline-guidance/early-years.

3 Session 2: Engaging parents and identifying next steps/ learning priorities

Practitioners had asked about involving parents in contributing to their child's learning journal and so this session included this topic.

Part 1: Involving parents in the OAP process

Parents have always been regarded as their child's first and most enduring educators. The revised EYFS 2012 strengthened the requirement to engage parents with their children's development and learning:

> The EYFS seeks to provide:
>
> - partnership working between practitioners and with parents and/or carers;
> - equality of opportunity and anti-discriminatory practice, ensuring that every child is included and supported.
>
> p. 2

> For children whose home language is not English, providers must take reasonable steps to provide opportunities for children to develop and use their home language in play and learning, supporting their language development at home.
>
> p. 6

> Each child must be assigned a key person (a safeguarding and welfare requirement – see paragraph 3.26). Providers must inform parents and/or carers of the name of the key person, and explain their role, when a child starts attending a setting. The key person must help ensure that every child's learning and care is tailored to meet their individual needs. The key person must seek to engage and support parents and/or carers in guiding their child's development at home. They should also help families engage with more specialist support if appropriate.
>
> p. 7

> Ongoing assessment (also known as formative assessment) is an integral part of the learning and development process. It involves practitioners observing children to understand their level of achievement, interests and learning styles, and to then shape learning experiences for each child reflecting those observations. In their interactions with children, practitioners should respond to their own day-to-day observations about children's progress, and observations that parents and carers share.
>
> p. 10

What kinds of information do we need to share?

Before the child is admitted:

- Parents' knowledge of their child and family – including significant events and important people in the child's life, their interests and experiences at home, any dietary, developmental or health needs, languages spoken etc.
- Information about the setting and the staff (including relevant policies) and what the child will experience – ask parents what they want to know (often they have further questions after the child has attended for a few weeks).

During the child's time in the setting:

- Daily exchanges of anything significant for the child, family or setting.
- What will be happening that day/week including information about meals.
- What the child experienced/learned, or is interested in, both in the setting and at home.
- Significant achievements for the child (sometimes called 'wow' moments), and any challenges that staff or parents are experiencing with the child's behaviour or development.
- The progress the child is making and any learning or development priorities.
- Parents' views of their child's experience.
- How children develop and learn most effectively (why certain approaches are more effective) and ways in which staff and parents can work together to support the child's development – it is particularly important to encourage and support parents to talk with their babies and young child at home. Useful information can be found at www.ican.org.uk and www.talkingpoint.org.uk.

Information sharing can include:

- informal and formal discussions between staff and parents;
- social events;
- sharing information through displays, written material, workshops, photos and video – using texts and email, if necessary, to ensure all parents can access information;
- valuing linguistic and cultural diversity and making information available in a range of languages;
- staff and parents contributing to child's record of development/portfolio.

The following sheet (next page) could be used to audit existing strategies for developing a partnership with parents and making plans to develop practice.

As a result of this session, practitioners set up 'Wow' boards where parents could jot down on the Post-it notes provided any development they had noticed in their child. Practitioners recorded for those parents who preferred to talk about their child. Some practitioners put up examples (or sent them home in a letter) to give parents ideas of the kinds of things they could include. It is essential that parents whose first language is not English are supported to contribute to, and feel involved with, their child's learning journey. Interpreters and translators may be needed to ensure equality of opportunity.

Auditing partnership with parents

Type of information sharing	In place	How effective?	To develop?
Meetings with individual parents (informal and formal)			
Social events			
Written/photographic/video information			
Valuing linguistic and cultural diversity			
Staff and parents contributing to child's learning journals			
Engaging parents in the setting			
Workshops on early learning and development			
Seeking parents' views			

Part 2: Identifying next steps

Many practitioners had been trying to identify a next step for every quick jotting and every longer observation and said they had found this daunting. They were reassured to hear that:

- it is usually necessary to have a number of observations of a child in order to be able to identify a clear learning priority or next step, and that
- not every observation leads to a next step.

On the training we discussed changing the language we use. Instead of writing 'Next Steps' at the bottom of observation pro formas, it was suggested that they try writing 'What next'. This was found to be very helpful, because it enabled practitioners to record what they would offer or provide for the child – or even leave it empty! We also discussed using the phrase 'learning priority' rather than next step. It was felt that the phrase next step implied that development and learning was like a ladder and that we had to be constantly trying to make children climb up another rung, when what they often needed was a broadening of experience to help them become more rounded learners. Many leaders commented that their staff found this change of language empowering and were consequently much more confident to plan for their key children. It was suggested that, when a small number of children are focused on each week and staff discuss them at the end of the week, this could be a good time to identify their learning priorities.

What is involved in identifying clear learning priorities (next steps)?

Some general points:

- Team work – everyone who knows the child should contribute observations and ideas not just the key person.
- Quality factual observations and valid/personalised assessments – which capture the unique child and focus on his/her strengths and interests.
- Raising questions as well as searching for answers – sometimes the evidence we collect for children raises questions that we might want to explore with other colleagues, with the child's parents and through making further observations.
- A good knowledge of child development and the ways in which one area of development impacts on other areas.

Learning priorities (next steps) can include:

- More of the same so that a child can practise and consolidate their learning – this is particularly important with children who are just beginning to grasp a concept, develop a new skill or demonstrate an attitude or learning disposition such as confidence or persistence.
- Broadening a child's experience by encouraging him/her to make a wider range of choices – sometimes this involves using their interests or preferred choices to introduce them to new experiences.
- Extending a particular interest or strength.
- Working on a different aspect of development in order to promote development in another area (e.g. working on language development to support development with behaviour or gross motor development to support development with mark-making).

- Sometimes (particularly in the short term) it is more about what adults need to provide or do for the child.

Learning priorities need to be:

- Written in clear language that all staff and parents can understand – jargon or general statements should be avoided (e.g. 'to develop communication skills' is not clear, but 'to be able to use some short phrases to express her needs and feelings' e.g. 'help please', 'I want . . .', 'play with me please' is clear).
- Realistic and achievable by that child in the time scale agreed.
- Be linked to clear strategies that all adults can follow at home and in the setting.

Strategies for supporting the child to achieve his/her learning priority need to:

- Take account of the child's interests and preferred ways of learning.
- Identify suitable motivating contexts/experiences that would enable the child to achieve the aim.
- Identify clearly what adults need to do (at home and in the setting) to support the child to achieve the next step/learning priority.

Identifying and recording learning priorities seemed to be particularly challenging for some practitioners, so during the last session of the course we revisited this and the following step by step guidelines were provided:

- Start with your factual knowledge of the child to identify progress made in the areas of learning and development (since last review), strengths and interests – the more you know about a child the easier it becomes to see what they need.
- Consider areas where less progress has been observed and think about why this is the case (it could be because adults haven't provided opportunities, or haven't noticed, and this may need to be addressed).
- Identify first whether the child is making good progress in each of the Prime Areas – if not, this has to be given priority.
- Identify any other needs you feel the child has – identify which of these will be addressed naturally through the everyday provision and teaching and which might need specific attention.
- Once you have decided which areas the child needs support with, you can then start thinking about what exactly you want the child to be able to do, or what you want her to know and understand.
- Write the learning priorities in clear language that all staff and parents can understand – start them with phrases related to learning such as I want A:

  to be able to . . . .
  to be . . . . (e.g. confident to)
  to know or understand . . . .
  to show awareness of . . . .

- Make your priorities specific, not general e.g. I want A to be confident to approach another child and ask them to play; or I want C to be able to tell a story for an adult to scribe or I want D to know how to use the woodwork tools safely etc. The priorities could also be written in the child's voice e.g. I want to be able to . . . , but, if this approach is taken, the child must be genuinely involved with the process.

- Think about the time scale and ensure that your priority is challenging enough for that length of time (i.e. not something the child could achieve by the next day/week).
- Once you are happy that you have a clear learning priority you can think about the strategies you need to use to ensure the child will be able to achieve it in that time scale.

This sheet, following page, (developed from Figure 6.4, Chapter 4 in *The Foundation Stage Teacher in Action* (third edition), Edgington 2004) can be used to record learning priorities for an individual child or could be used to record for a number of individual children in a key worker group. There is a column on the far right that enables adults to consider whether any other children in the setting would benefit from similar support.

Setting based follow-up work

Participants were asked to introduce focused observation of a small number of children per week in their setting, to review the children at the end of the week and to complete a learning priority sheet for them. They were asked to involve their colleagues in this.

Feedback from participants, who had not made focused observations before, indicated that they had found doing so extremely useful in getting to know the children in depth as individuals. Many of them said they were surprised by what they saw and heard when the child was involved in child-initiated play and everyone recognised how useful these observations were for identifying the needs of and supporting the most challenging children and those who can be overlooked within a busy setting because they are quiet and don't demand attention.

Reception teachers were encouraged to write the child's age in years and months on their focused observations, as a regular reminder of which children were the youngest in the group. They were encouraged not to use the phrases 'less able' or 'low ability' in relation to reception class children and to replace these phrases with 'less experienced'. This is because many of the children, who appear to achieve less well, actually have less life experience and/or are up to a whole year younger than others in their group and simply need more experience or more time. Other children are learning English as an additional language and can express their learning more effectively in their first language. It is important not to limit children's progress by assigning inappropriate labels to them – even very young children know when they are seen as being inferior in some way to others in their group and this can become a self-fulfilling prophecy for them.

Sheet for recording individual learning priorities

Child's name	What are the child's strengths, interests? How/where does s/he prefer to learn?	How would you like the child to develop over the next month or so? Start your next steps with I want A to be/ be able to/to know/ to understand etc.	What will you provide and do to support the child to achieve this? You may want to use the child's interests and strengths to introduce new learning.	Are there other children who would benefit from similar support?

This group of boys love to play with the cars and blocks. They often choose to play in this area as soon as they arrive at the beginning of the session. The observations and assessments have revealed that their next steps include developing their fine motor skills, particularly triangulating and pincer grip. We wanted to increase their self chosen opportunities for using pens for mark making, emergent writing and using scissors in their play. We knew that these could be linked to their interest in this type of play with cars and construction.

Tools for mark making and creative opportunities were already available in that area but we decided that as we played alongside the children we would introduce the idea of labelling or enhancing using the tools as a natural complement to the direction of their play – we didn't want to impose or re-direct necessarily, but extend their ideas and offer possibilities.

As the boys built car parks for their cars, it was a natural suggestion to add the idea of buying tickets for the cars and also to label them so they could be found easily.

The boys decided to write on numbers, tickets and names and then decided to cut them up to stick them on to the cars. This not only promoted the desired next steps as we had hoped, but also promoted a great deal of planning and decision making too.

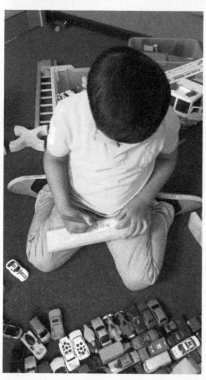

Days later, in their child-initiated play, the impact of the adult support was evident as the children chose to label their constructions independently. They chose to stick masking tape on to the blocks to write on them. This became a prominent feature of their constructions from that point forward. Adults still made interventions to support the next steps. Another result was that the boys were more pro-active in bringing extra resources from the mark-making table to the floor play area. After this, the boys also began to draw, create products and write at the mark-making table as part of their freely chosen self-initiated play.

4 years 6 months to 4 years 9 months

The children are in their last term before starting school. This group of children are articulate and confident speakers for their age and stage of development. The environment is rich with language experiences that support attention and listening, understanding and speaking. The daily routines and experiences of the children have musical, sound discrimination and tuning in opportunities threaded through them. This group have good phonic awareness for their age/stage. They are already aware of linking letters to sounds and often point out familiar meaningful letters in the indoor environment.

The next steps for the children here include beginning to hear initial sounds in words; some can begin to blend and to begin to use letters in their writing to represent sounds in words. The weather is good and the children love to be outside and so the staff have painted pebbles with some of the letters the children know. The pebbles have been left on the tree rings, near to pens and paper on clipboards. Other natural pebbles are around for transport and for painting.

The children discover the pebbles and begin to talk to each other about letters they know, letters in their names and they discuss patterns on the pebbles.

One child is immediately interested in writing letters on the clipboards. Others related the letters to sounds at the beginning of words, reflecting some of their adult-initiated experiences.

They experiment with putting letters together to see if they make a word. An adult joins in to suggest some words that can be formed easily using the letters. 'Can you make . . . cat?' 'What about . . . hat?' The children work together with initial support and find ways to make the words.

When the adult has left, they continue to build words and then move on to draw pebbles and to use the pebble-letters to write words on their boards.

Ages 3 years 4 months to 4 years 1 month

The children have just been involved in a storytelling session where they helped Santa work out what is written on his list so that he can deliver the correct present to the correct person. After storytelling the adult invites the children to think about what they would like to do now. From observational assessments a number of children had next steps that included playing collaboratively with peers and also some had next steps that involved aspects of exploring mathematical concepts such as space, position, size and shape in their play.

One child says he wants to build Santa's sleigh from the wooden blocks and the children with identified next steps for collaboration and shape/space were asked if they would like to play too – they all enthusiastically agreed. An adult initially helped less experienced children join in with the group play in the first instance and then stepped back as the children were guided and supported by their more experienced peers.

For a sustained period, the children were engaged in creating the sleigh and as the construction evolved, children became engaged finding people (small figures) to go on the sleigh and presents to add. All the children were involved and engaged and those children identified as needing encouragement to become engaged in play with peers, were observed to do so, and often through the invitation of more experienced others.

An adult re-joined play; she asked about who the figures were and where the presents would go, would they fall out when it flies? 'Tell me about…' As the adult commented on and described the sleigh in her commentary, she added the vocabulary of positional language and language to describe the shape/position/size of the blocks, enclosures and towers.

References

DFE, *Early Years Foundation Stage Statutory Framework* (EYFS), 2012, DFE.
Edgington, M., *The Foundation Stage Teacher in Action* (third edition), 2004, Paul Chapman Publishing.

4 Session 3: From observation and assessment to planning

The third session started with a recap on identifying and recording learning priorities. Many practitioners find this challenging and it is useful to spend some staff meeting time working on this together.

This Progress Review offers an example that teams could use at a staff meeting to work together to identify a clear learning priority for a child and some strategies that would help her achieve this. The Progress Review Sheet is on page 36.

Planning for young children

The EYFS reminds us that when we are developing a curriculum for young children we need to consider:

- **child development** – the development of each unique individual including feelings, dispositions and attitudes, self-help skills, relationships, language, physical abilities and thinking skills;
- **how young children learn best** (both young children in general and individuals in your group) – including the characteristics of effective learning (EYFS 2012, pp. 6–7 and *Development Matters*, pp. 6–7);
- **what they need to learn** – their learning priorities.

Planning is essential to ensure that:

All children:

- can operate as self-motivated independent learners and can initiate their own learning – they need to be taught how to use the environment and resources independently and responsibly during the settling in period;
- gain relevant meaningful experiences that connect with their interests and life experience;
- are offered equal opportunities and are enabled to reach their full potential;
- have access to a broad experience, which meets their needs and covers all areas of learning over time;
- have access to adult time and support.

All adults:

- understand how all experiences in and out of doors can support children's learning, and are able to extend learning;
- can respond effectively to spontaneous interests and happenings – for example, you can plan and prepare in advance a box of resources to bring out to explore predictable interests such as the force of the wind on a windy day, or a festival or the new babies several children have at home;

Progress review sheet

Child's name: N

Date:

Personal, social and emotional development	Communication and language	Physical development
N self-registers and separates from her mum with confidence. She takes children by the hand and draws them into her play. She shows interest in what others are doing and sometimes imitates. She is motivated to choose and take part in a wide range of experiences indoors and outside but her favourite area is the home corner. She knows where equipment goes and takes a full part in tidying up.	N is motivated to communicate with adults and the other children. She expresses feelings/ needs through gesture, sounds and one or two recognisable words. She can get frustrated and scream if others don't understand. She can repeat words and can imitate the intonation patterns in a conversation, e.g. when on the home corner phone.	N runs, climbs and jumps confidently and can ride a tricycle steering well. She is willing to have a go with new equipment and tools. She can use scissors with adult support and holds a crayon in her fist (palmer grasp) to draw lines and circular shapes. She can manage her own personal needs – including putting on and fastening up coat, going to the toilet and using cutlery to eat lunch.

Mathematics	Understanding the world	Literacy	Expressive arts and design
N can sort and match items when tidying away. She joins in with counting during action rhymes.	N knows her way around the nursery and shows understanding of the pattern of the day.	She sits attentively at story time, tries to join in with books, rhymes and songs.	N re-enacts domestic activities in the home corner. She willingly explores new media and materials.

Interests

Particular strengths:

Blank Progress Review sheet that can be adapted by each setting.

Progress review sheet

Child's name: Date:

Personal, social and emotional development	Communication and language	Physical development

Mathematics	Understanding the world	Literacy	Expressive arts and design

Interests

Particular strengths:

- have time to work in depth with the children;
- work consistently as a team.

The provision indoors and outside:

- is of a high quality and gives children access to cross-curricular learning;
- is well organised and maintained;
- is regularly reviewed and developed;
- is developed in response to observed needs and seasonal or community events.

These reasons should inform our approach to planning and our practice should ensure they are achieved. Because planning needs to be much more individual for babies and toddlers than for 3–5 year olds, and, because the challenges faced by reception teachers were different from those faced by practitioners working in day care settings, this session gave general guidance on planning rather than a definitive model. Each practitioner was expected to take responsibility (with support from their support teacher) for developing their own approach. Many practitioners want to be given formats for short term planning, but this rarely works, as each setting is different and needs an approach that works for that setting and for the practitioners in it. The amount of recording also needs to be considered. The most effective plans are those made and acted upon immediately in response to what is observed and these may never be written down or written as quick jotting after the event. Less is certainly more in the case of weekly planning for Early Years' settings! However, it takes a high level of skill to plan responsively and those practitioners that are able to do this are supported by the attention they have given to other levels of planning.

Continuous provision outdoors

Stages in planning

Long term planning provides an overview and framework that guides the work of the setting and includes:

- statutory frameworks;
- national and Local Authority Guidelines that practitioners can use as and when they need additional support;
- setting booklet and policy statements relevant to early learning and development, which should determine the ethos and practice within the setting;
- careful planning of the learning environment – with a clear view about what children can learn when they are accessing different provision areas indoors and outside;
- rotas and routines – setting out how time and adults are managed.

All of these need occasional review, but are developed for the long term.

Quality child-initiated learning is dependent on an excellent environment and this needs to be very carefully planned (see *An Enabling Environment – Steps we have Taken* by Hampshire County Council 2011. See also the work of Community Playthings (www.communityplaythings.co.uk) and Early Excellence (www.earlyexcellence.com).

Early Excellence has, for many years through their training and interactive environment, encouraged practitioners to plan for:

- **Continuous provision** – provision areas and core resources indoors and outside always available in the same place (planned in the long term). This gives children a sense of security and a feeling of ownership of their environment.
- **Enhanced provision/new stimulus** – resources added for a short time to develop interest or in response to existing interests (planned in the medium and short term).

The following sheet on page 42 could be used for planning a continuous provision area:

Continuous provision indoors

Continuous provision plan for: (e.g. home corner)

What will the children learn in this area?			Which resources need to be available every day? (include number of items where relevant)
PSE	CL	PD	
UW	L	M	EAD	

What does the adult need to model?

Medium term planning

Some practitioners feel there is no need for medium term planning and it is certainly true that planning for babies and toddlers is best done spontaneously in response to the children's developmental needs and interests.

For 2–5-year-olds medium term topic led planning, where everything stems from a narrow topic, is inappropriate, as it is not flexible enough to take account of children's spontaneous interests and may only appeal to some members of the group.

There has been some confusion about planning from children's interests with some practitioners believing they can no longer introduce new interests or experiences. This is clearly not the case, as all young children lack life experience and there are many things that are new to them. Effective planning caters for their existing experience and interests, but also introduces them to new interests.

Medium term planning for 2–5-year-olds therefore focuses on looking ahead to prepare resources etc. for the new interests/learning that will be developed over the next few weeks – these must be influenced by observations of children's interests and needs, but should also include new adult initiated interests to broaden children's experience – e.g. in the spring/summer planting, growing, harvesting, preparing, cooking and eating fruit and vegetables is an entitlement that many children will not yet know they enjoy, as they have not had this experience before.

Medium term planning involves looking ahead over the next few weeks and considering:

- how children's current interests could be developed and extended;
- how seasonal and community events (e.g. a building site nearby, or a celebration such as new babies) could be used to enhance children's learning;
- some of the experiences and resources that could be offered to promote learning (including visits and visitors).

Medium term planning highlights **possibilities** and enables practitioners to access resources and plan outings and visitors in good time.

Enhancements based on interests

Settling in framework

When children join a setting for the first time it is vital that they are supported through the settling in period.

The sheet on page 47 could provide **a starting point** for developing a medium term plan for settling in, which could also be used as an assessment tool to ensure all children are settling well. It needs to be edited and developed to reflect different age groups and the characteristics of different settings.

Setting based task

Using the notes above, work as a team to reflect on what you have in place that you would call:

- long term planning?
- medium term planning (including settling in framework)?

How effective are these and how well used? Do you feel you need to develop them?

Short term planning

Highlights the interests/learning that will be focused on that week/day. It needs to:

- reflect the previous week's/day's observations of the children's interests and needs (including the children you have focused on the previous week);
- be flexible enough to enable immediate responses;
- reflect the fact that much planning is spontaneous and have space to record spontaneous learning;
- leave time for adults to observe and then support and extend child-initiated learning – adult-led sessions must not be allowed to dominate.

Short term plans work best if they are developed as the week progresses and the younger the children the more they need an individual approach to planning.

Short term planning should include, but may not all be recorded:

- specific development and learning objectives, which will be given priority (based on children's needs and interests) – these come from children's learning priorities;
- additional provision or resources to be added to the continuous provision (indoors and outside) to respond to interests and to encourage child-initiated learning;
- adult-initiated experiences such as cooking, gardening, teaching how to use equipment, as well as planned involvement in provision areas (e.g. to model play);
- what roles adults will take (including who will have time to observe and get involved in child-initiated play);
- children to be focused on for observation;
- an evaluation section.

As stated earlier, no set pro formas for planning were given, as it was felt more helpful for practitioners to work from what they already used and improve the content of those sheets. The case studies show clearly how this strategy empowered leaders to innovate and develop their own approach with their team. Many practitioners in nurseries and pre-schools recognised that their short term planning focused mainly on activities and experiences rather than on development and learning. Reception teachers, on the other hand, found they often spend too much time directing the children rather than observing, supporting and extending their child-initiated learning.

The following approach to weekly planning was suggested as it focuses on children's existing interests, as well as enabling adults to introduce new experiences and learning opportunities:

- Think about what you want/need to include this/next week, informed by:
  - your medium term plan (for those working with 2–5-year-olds);
  - learning or interests started the previous week;
  - learning priorities identified for the focus children;
  - general learning needs of children,
    and identify a few (not too many!) clear learning intentions;
- Think about how you will need to enhance provision areas indoors and outside to support and promote child-initiated learning (including any visits/visitors).
- Identify adult initiated experiences you wish to offer (indoors and outside) and decide when these need to happen and who will lead them – remember these can include planned participation in provision areas.

There should be a clear plan for Monday but only a skeleton plan for the rest of the week, which can be added to on a daily basis in response to observations. Practitioners were asked to try this approach between sessions 3 and 4 with support from a linked teacher.

The session ended with a discussion of the follow-up work to be carried out between sessions:

- Think about your current planning and identify questions/issues you want to raise at the next session.
- Review how observation and assessment procedures have developed in your setting. Carry out at least one progress review and set learning priorities for one child and come prepared to share achievements/any queries.

There was also a reminder that 'All planning starts with observing children in order to understand and consider their current interests, development and learning.' EYFS Principles into Practice card 3.1.

Settling in framework: Some starting points

Children need to learn:

PSE	CL	PD
To separate from main carer with confidence	To want to communicate	To be willing to explore the environment through gross and fine motor activity
To be motivated to take part in experiences indoors and outside	To be able to express feelings and needs	To be willing to take a risk
To manage own personal needs	To know some vocabulary of the setting (including names of adults and children)	To manage their own basic hygiene and personal needs
To know the setting's expectations		
To be able to select and return resources		
	L	
	To show interest/ enjoyment in books, stories, rhymes and songs	

Understanding the world	Mathematics	EAD
To know their way round the environment	To show an interest in sorting, counting when playing and tidying up	To be motivated to try new creative experiences
To know the daily routine	To be able to sort and match when tidying away	To be able to represent ideas using a range of media
To be curious and use senses to explore		

It was the children's first day at nursery. We knew from home visits, visits to the settings and transition information that the children in this small group were interested in active play outdoors, building and constructing. With this in mind we enhanced this area of our outdoor provision with some of the creative construction already set up to offer a channel for water flow into a trough near to the open construction bunker that houses a variety of equipment (role play resources, building blocks, cushions, tools and crates etc). This would be a starting point for the children who had not yet learned what resources we have or the play possibilities they could create.

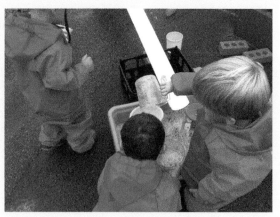

We supported the children in accessing the wet weather clothes and boots as they chose to play in this area. As play progressed the children realised that other resources nearby could also be incorporated in to their play and so began to explore their own ideas.

The provision of water as an open ended experience engaged the children for a long period as they explore the movement of water and used available resources to move water from the trough to the top of the guttering.

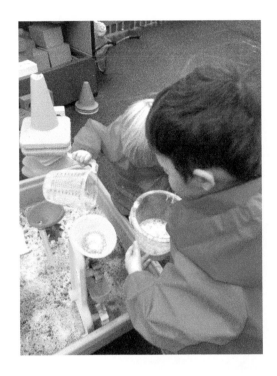

The children spontaneously accessed the role play resources and some began to take on particular roles of builders making and mending the water system.

As water was spilled an adult supported play to offer the idea of getting more water 'Would you like bubbles added this time? What colour would you like?' The children accompanied the adult to find out how to access more water. The adult also suggested the addition of the waterproof coats to prevent clothes getting too wet as they transported the water and supported the children in putting on their coats.

On their first day at nursery the group of children were completely and effectively engaged in their play for a very long period. They had begun to explore, in depth, the possibilities of just one area of the continuous provision outdoors and how they could continue to select and manipulate resources to follow their ideas. Their first day offered experiences that interested them, motivated them and provided excitement for the possibilities for play the following day.

References

Early Education, *Development Matters,* 2012, Early Education.
Hampshire County Council, *An Enabling Environment – Steps we have Taken,* 2011, Hampshire County Council.

5 Session 4: Recognising the Characteristics of Effective Learning

In response to requests from reception teachers, the final session took as its main focus the Characteristics of Effective Learning, which are highlighted in the revised EYFS 2012:

> In planning and guiding children's activities, practitioners must reflect on the different ways that children learn and reflect these in their practice. Three characteristics of effective teaching and learning are:
>
> - **playing and exploring** – children investigate and experience things, and 'have a go';
> - **active learning** – children concentrate and keep on trying if they encounter difficulties, and enjoy achievements; and
> - **creating and thinking critically** – children have and develop their own ideas, make links between ideas, and develop strategies for doing things.
>
> pp. 6–7

We looked at these in some depth to ensure that the practitioners understood the importance of these characteristics and were able to recognise how children demonstrated them. We also highlighted that they are interrelated and interdependent, with play often providing the vehicle for children to demonstrate the other characteristics.

The session drew together and highlighted some material related to each of the characteristics, which practitioners could draw on when justifying their practice and also when assessing children demonstrating the characteristics.

The Characteristics of Effective Learning are important because they:

- help develop positive attitudes and dispositions;
- enable children to show us their needs, interests and preferences, feelings and ideas – we can build on these and make learning personally relevant to each child;
- enable children to transfer adult-led learning and make it their own;

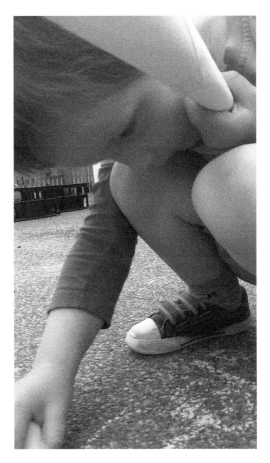

Involvement and concentrating

● encourage children to stretch themselves and meet their own learning needs – they often surprise us when they are leading their own learning.

Active learning

Creativity and critical thinking

Playing and exploring

Play is a particularly important vehicle for learning for young children. This wonderful quotation found on the website http://quixoteconsulting.com/Blog/2013/09/20/play-and-learning-quotes-part-5/ (along with many others) sums up why it is so crucial in helping children to become lifelong learners:

> It's not so much what children learn through play, but what they won't learn if we don't give them the chance to play. Many functional skills like literacy and arithmetic can be learned either through play or through instruction – the issue is the amount of stress on the child. However, many coping skills like compassion, self-regulation, self-confidence, the habit of active engagement, and the motivation to learn and be literate cannot be instructed. They can only be learned through self-directed experience (i.e. play).
>
> Susan J. Oliver (of the organisation Playing for Keeps)

It is important to note that, in their play, children often demonstrate all the other characteristics.

Mastering new skills

Lilian Katz (2011) identified 4 types of learning goal: knowledge/understanding, skills, dispositions, which she defines as 'habits of mind with intentions and motives (not attitudes)' (p. 121), and feelings. She suggests that it is not possible to instruct children to develop dispositions and feelings – children learn them from experience and from the people around them. It is, however, possible to damage children's dispositions by inappropriate instruction.

Katz's work reminds us that:

- Children can **know** how to read and write and have the **skill** to do both, but may not **feel** good about themselves as readers and writers and may not have the **disposition** to be a reader and writer.
- Practitioners need to pay attention to all 4 learning goals if children are to make lasting progress.
- We need to observe to ensure we notice children who are losing confidence and becoming unmotivated.

The National Strategies in their publication *Learning Playing and Interacting* (2009) provided a useful definition of play:

> **Play** is freely chosen by the child, and is under the control of the child. The child decides how to play, how long to sustain the play, what the play is about, and who to play with. There are many forms of play, but it is usually highly creative, open-ended and imaginative. It requires active engagement of the players, and can be deeply satisfying.

p. 10

Taking risks and being willing to have a go   Focussing on what you are doing

When children are playing they explore:

- feelings;
- materials;
- ideas;
- relationships and roles (including language of roles);
- connections between one experience and another;
- signs and symbols.

Finding out and exploring

Sharing experiences

In their play children represent ideas, objects, people and environments. Play can be solitary or include others (observing, playing in parallel or playing collaboratively). This booklet also highlights the dispositions that can be promoted by play.

Enjoying together

Play can help children to develop these positive dispositions for learning:

- finding an interest;
- being willing to explore, experiment and try things out;
- knowing how and where to seek help;
- being inventive – creating problems, and finding solutions;
- being flexible – testing and refining solutions;
- being engaged and involved – concentrating, sustaining interest, persevering with a task, even when it is challenging;
- making choices and decisions;
- making plans and knowing how to carry them out;
- playing and working collaboratively with peers and adults;
- managing self, managing others;
- developing 'can-do' orientations to learning;
- being resilient – finding alternative strategies if things don't always go as planned;
- understanding the perspectives and emotions of other people.

Learning Playing and Interacting (2009) pp. 10–11

Planning and carrying out the plan

Vivian Gussin Paley, in her inspiring book *The Boy Who Would be a Helicopter*, writes:

'We were taught to say that play is the work of children. But watching and listening to them, I saw that play was nothing less than Truth and Life'

p. 17

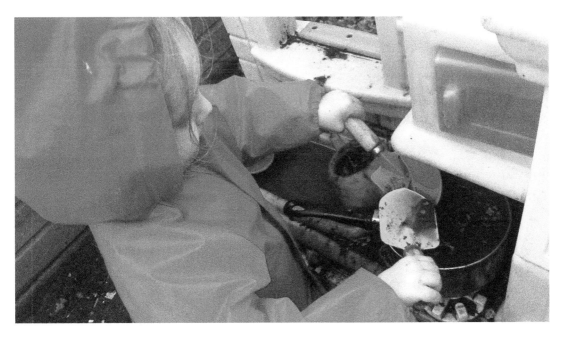

Finding new ways to do things

Exploring involves having the confidence to:

- use all senses;
- watch what others do and how they behave and then imitate – pretending and representing;
- interact with materials, objects and people;
- take risks and accept a challenge
- raise questions and seek out answers – 'what does this feel like/do?'; 'what can I do with it?'; etc.;
- engage and communicate with others both verbally and non-verbally.

Some children arrive at settings lacking the confidence to explore (especially if they risk getting dirty) and take risks. Some may have been inhibited by adults around them and some may have cautious personalities. It is the role of the practitioner to support children to try new things and to move beyond their comfort zone.

Facing challenges and adapting plans

Active learning

Active learning is not just about physical activity. It involves:

- **Physical engagement** – sensory exploration, hands-on experience, movement, transference of materials and ideas from one context to another;
- **Emotional engagement** – motivation, curiosity, confidence, self-belief, empathy, resilience, pride;
- **Intellectual engagement** – concentration, thinking, encountering contradictions and problems and persisting to address these;
- **Social engagement** – children learning alongside and from others (both other children and adults), both within and outside of the setting. This social engagement which requires sharing, turn-taking, collaborating, working as a team member and leader, negotiating, resolving conflict and many other social skills is particularly challenging for young children.

Learning from others

Often children demonstrate a number of types of engagement within one experience.

Creating and thinking critically

Dictionary definitions of creativity include:

- 'having the ability to create';
- 'originality of thought';
- 'having or showing imagination';
- 'sophisticated bending of the rules or conventions'.

Having your own ideas

Tina Bruce reminds us that young children's creations are mostly '*of the everyday kind*' (see *Cultivating Creativity*, 2004 Hodder and Stoughton, p. 135) and that creativity is part of virtually every subject discipline, not just the arts.

We need to recognise that you need to be creative to be:

- A mathematician
- A scientist
- A writer
- An artist
- An ICT specialist
- A gymnast or dancer
- A musician
- A gardener

- A chef
- A doctor
- An actor
- A hairdresser
- A mechanic
- A teacher/practitioner
- A plumber or carpenter

and lots of other things!

The idea that we need to support and extend children's thinking came from the '*Researching Effective Pedagogy in the Early Years*' (REPEY) project, which concluded:

> adult-child interactions that involve some element of 'sustained shared thinking' or what Bruner has termed 'joint involvement episodes' may be especially valuable in terms of children's learning.
>
> REPEY 2002 p. 10

Open ended experiences

Sustained shared thinking means:

> An episode in which two or more
> individuals 'work together' in an
> intellectual way to solve a prob-
> lem, clarify a concept, evaluate
> activities, extend a narrative etc.
> Both parties must contribute to
> the thinking and it must develop
> and extend.
>
> REPEY 2002 p. 8

Young children show their think-
ing through:

- their interactions with objects and materials;
- their behaviours or pre-occupations within self-chosen activity (includ-ing their schema);
- their questions (non-verbal or verbal);
- their verbal interactions with others;
- their mark making.

Being involved and concentrating

We see they are powerful thinkers if we are willing to try to understand them.

> In his mental model of the world, there are a great many gaps that he might sense, but he is not able to put these into words. A child just feels a gap in his mind, like a missing piece in a jigsaw puzzle. But when, through his experiences, one way or another, along comes the piece of information that fits the gap, it's pulled in there as if by a magnet. I think we've all experienced this.
>
> *Learning all the Time*, John Holt 1989 Education Now Publishing Co-operative p.153

The Characteristics of Effective Learning are most likely to be demonstrated:

- when children are initiating their own learning;
- when children have adults or more experienced peers to act as role models and to provide challenge – both by adding resources and by interacting;
- within meaningful, real life experiences that motivate and inspire children and that are challenging but achievable for them;
- when children receive personal encouragement and positive feedback from others e.g. telling a child 'you worked really hard to solve that problem'.

Planning and exploring: engagement

Avoid:

- Over-planning and over-directing – you need time to observe, listen and reflect.
- Telling or showing children what to do with open-ended materials and experiences – children need to be free to develop their own ideas of how to use things like boxes, shells, pebbles, tins, paint etc.
- Providing models for children to copy or fill in e.g. handwriting practice sheets, colouring in, filling in adult drawn shapes or making adult-designed models.

- A daily routine that is fragmented with little time to work in depth – including too little time out of doors for deep involvement. Children cannot develop their ideas fully if they are constantly interrupted. Try to ensure that children can return to the same provision over a number of days or even weeks.

Enjoy achieving what you set out to achieve

Setting-based follow-up work

Make video clips of children playing and ask staff to make observations and then identify the Characteristics of Effective Learning that were being demonstrated and how they were supported (by the environment and by other children and/or an adult) to display these characteristics.

- To what extent do staff members see the same things?
- How could they ensure all children have the chance to demonstrate the Characteristics of Effective Learning?

Playing with what you know well

The training finished with a reminder:

- Best practice has altered very little over many years.
- Confident practitioners have strong beliefs, based on their knowledge and experience, and breed confidence in others.
- Working with young children should be fascinating and joyful (it should not be a chore!).

> Early years educators play a critical role in young children's learning. It is within their power to encourage feelings of fun and discovery in learning on the one hand or of dull drudgery on the other.
> Rumbold Report 1990 HMSO p. 36 par 4

Keeping on trying

Showing high levels of energy

References and further reading

Bruce, T., *Cultivating Creativity in Babies, Toddlers and Young Children*, 2004 (2nd edition 2011) Hodder and Stoughton.

Costello, P., *Thinking Skills and Early Childhood Education*, 2000, David Fulton.

DFE, *Early Years Foundation Stage Statutory Framework*, 2012, DFE.

Ephgrave, A., *The Reception Year in Action*, 2nd edition, 2012, Routledge.

Gussin Paley, V., *The Boy Who Would be a Helicopter*, 1991, Harvard University Press.

Holt, J., *Learning all the Time,* 1989, Education Now.

Katz, L., Current Perspectives on the Early Years Curriculum, in *Too Much Too Soon: Early Learning and the Erosion of Childhood (Early Years)*, ed. House, R., 2011, Hawthorn Press.

National Strategies, Early Years, *Learning Playing and Interacting*, 2009, DCSF Publications.

Nutbrown, C., *Threads of Thinking*, 4th edition, 2011, Sage.

The Rumbold Report – Starting with Quality The Report of the Committee of Inquiry into the Quality of the Educational Experience offered to 3 and 4 year olds, chaired by Mrs Angela Rumbold CBE MP, 1990.

Siraj-Blatchford, I., Sylva, K., Muttock, S., Gilden, R. and Bell, D., *Researching Effective Pedagogy in the Early Years*, 2002, DFES.

Stewart, N., *How Children Learn: the Characteristics of Effective Learning*, 2011, Early Education, p. 78.

Training materials

Dowling, M., *Supporting Young Children's Sustained Shared Thinking, and 'Exploring Young Children's Thinking Through their Self-chosen Activities'*, 2005, Early Education.

The Observation Series DVDs and *Playing and Learning at School* DVD, available from www.sirenfilms.co.uk.

6 Twilight session for head teachers

During the sessions with reception teachers, it became clear that they would need support from senior managers to implement the training. Reception teachers can feel under 'top-down' pressure to work in ways that are not consistent with good Early Years practice and the statutory EYFS framework and head teachers, who are under pressure to raise standards, may not have experience of Early Years teaching and may therefore not be aware of the best way of supporting their reception staff. We therefore decided to run a 2-hour twilight session for head teachers and senior leaders in schools. The main content of this session is included below (NB some of the content is deliberately the same as the reception teachers' experience on the course).

The session started with some general points about assessing young children's learning and development:

- The period from birth to 5 is the time of most rapid growth and development in a human being's life – a few days or weeks can make a huge difference in terms of development.
- All areas of learning and development are equally important and interdependent, but the prime areas in the revised EYFS underpin everything else.
- Young children develop at different rates.
- Their development is dependent on experiences they have had.
- Each child's development follows a unique pathway and is not linear.

It was stressed that a few weeks' difference in age or life experience can make a big difference at this time in a child's life. There is a real danger that summer born children, or those who have missed out on important experiences, will be wrongly labelled as 'less able' or as having special educational needs (see Sykes et al., 2009 and Maclure and Jones, 2009).

The new 'expected' level in the revised EYFS is problematic because:

- Some children are virtually a year younger than others when they are assessed for the EYFS Profile and will be at a disadvantage.
- It sets the bar significantly higher than it was under the previous EYFS Profile, when a good level of development was deemed to be the achievement of a point score of 6 (to achieve the entire goal required a point score of 8) – the expected level requires children to achieve the whole goal.
- Some of the goals have been made much harder e.g. for Mathematics. The writing goal remains optimistic for many children, with national statistics showing that boys find this goal particularly challenging.

There is a real danger that children who cannot cope with these 'expectations' will be given more of what they cannot do, at the expense of time being spent on the things they really need to learn, and they may become dispirited and switched off from learning.

Effective assessment in the Early Years

The reliability of any assessment of young children is dependent on:

- **Relationships** – the child needs to trust their key practitioners in order to show their full capabilities – assessments made before children have fully settled into school and formed positive relationships with their teacher and teaching assistant will always be unreliable.
- **Environment and context** – children can show some attitudes, skills and understanding in one environment or context but not necessarily in another. The EYFS Profile handbook states that children should be able to demonstrate their learning in child-initiated contexts.
- **Being based on factual, un-biased observations** – observation is the only way to really tune into each unique child.

The EYFS Profile handbook states:

> Reliable and accurate assessment at the end of the EYFS is underpinned by the following principles:
>
> - Reliable and accurate assessment is based primarily on the practitioner's knowledge of the child gained predominantly from observation and interaction in a range of daily activities and events.
> - Responsible pedagogy must be in place so that the provision enables each child to demonstrate their learning and development fully.
> - Embedded learning is identified by assessing what a child can do consistently and independently in a range of everyday situations.
> - An effective assessment presents a holistic view of a child's learning and development.
> - Accurate assessments take account of contributions from a range of perspectives including the child, their parents and other relevant adults.
>
> p. 8

> A child's embedded learning and secure development are demonstrated without the need for overt adult support. Where learning is secure it is likely that children often initiate the use of that learning. Judgements about this are made through observing behaviour that a child demonstrates consistently and independently, in a range of situations. Attainment in this context will assure practitioners of the child's confidence and ownership of the specific knowledge, skill or concept being assessed. Skilful interactions with adults and learning which is supported by them are necessary on the journey to embedding skills and knowledge.
>
> p. 10

These points are valid regardless of how assessment policy develops in the future. At the time of writing, it is clear that the government intends to introduce a new baseline assessment or test at the beginning of the reception year.

Early years practitioners know that baseline assessment is unlikely to be valid or reliable until the child is well settled into the class, and unless the assessment is based on observation of the child in everyday activities.

The importance of effective observation

The head teachers were then provided with the same input as the teachers regarding the importance of observation and how to make and recognise effective observations i.e.
Observation is essential because it helps us to:

- Focus on children as individuals, identifying their starting points (what they can do), strengths, interests, schema (repeated patterns of behaviour such as transporting or positioning) and learning styles as well as their development and learning.
- See each child's personal experience of the setting (the received experience as opposed to the offered experience). It is essential to ensure that all children can find things in the setting that connect with their interest and life experience.
- Raise questions about children's experience and learning, the quality of provision and of adult interactions (challenging assumptions) – observation should be used to help us improve the environment and our interactions with the children.
- Share factual information with colleagues and parents – for example, it is much less threatening to share facts about what the child did, than to share a judgement on a child's behaviour.
- Plan relevant, motivating developmentally appropriate experiences for each child.

What do we mean by observation and what kinds of observation do we need to make?

When we observe, we watch carefully and listen carefully and capture the facts of what we see the child do and what we hear the child say. We may capture the facts in our minds, on paper (a quick jotting or a longer narrative piece), in an annotated photo or by collecting and annotating the child's mark-making. Video and audio materials are other ways of capturing facts.
A factual quick jotting:

Amir   Context: *Alone in the home corner*

Took a pan to the cooker and selected a spoon from the cutlery tray. Said to me 'me make soup'.

(First time he spoke in English to an adult – children had made soup the previous day.)

A factual longer observation:

G. enters the room, says 'bye' to her mum and goes straight across to the cupboard where games are stored. She selects the texture dominoes and puts them on the floor. She places 2 chairs facing each other near the dominoes. She then goes to the creative area and chooses a thin brush from a pot of assorted brushes. She returns to the dominoes and calls to J. 'Let's do face painting, what d'you want on your face?' J. replies 'tiger', sits on chair and G. selects a rusty coloured shape on a domino and pretends to paint J.'s face. G. then says 'Your turn now, I want to be a clown' and gives J. the brush. They continue taking turns in play for 15 minutes.

Assessments need to:

- be based on factual observations – often more than one observation is required to make a secure assessment;
- focus on the prime and specific areas of learning and also on how the child demonstrates the Characteristics of Effective Learning (EYFS pages 6–7 and *Development Matters* pages 6–7).

The key messages given to the reception teachers on the course were shared with the head teachers:

- Observations must be factual – not adult interpretations or judgements. (See EYFS Profile exemplification material for good examples.)
- The only statutory requirements for assessment in late 2014, the EYFS are the Progress Check at 2 years of age and the EYFS Profile at the end of reception year – where the teacher makes a best fit judgement about whether the child has achieved the 'expected' level, or is emerging or exceeding this level, and reports on how the child has demonstrated the Characteristics of Effective Learning. In September 2016, it is likely that a baseline assessment/test will be introduced.
- *Development Matters*, and the more recent *Early Years Outcomes*, are non-statutory guidance – they should not be used as a checklist and children do not have to achieve all the points in any age band. It is suggested that practitioners might use it to make ongoing 'best fit' assessments when carrying out progress reviews, but they do not have to.
- It is not possible or desirable to write a next step for every observation. We discussed the phrase 'learning priorities' (as an alternative to 'next steps') and suggested these could be identified when half-termly/termly progress reviews are carried out.
- When children are not secure in a Prime Area of learning and development, this needs to be given high priority.
- The quality of the learning environment indoors and outside determines the quality of child-initiated learning – it acts as an additional teacher and continuous provision needs careful planning.
- Topics planned too rigidly, without reference to children's current interest and needs, make it difficult for teachers to develop a responsive curriculum. It was suggested that a number of 'centres of interest' are decided on half-termly and that these include interests initiated by the children, but also adult-initiated interests to broaden children's experience.
- Planning must be flexible so that it can be informed by on-going observation.

In best Early Years practice practitioners often:

- observe what the children are doing;
- assess their needs and interests;
- plan spontaneously how we could address their needs or extend their interests, and;
- act on this plan **in the space of a few minutes or within the same day.**

Recording often has to be done retrospectively – and this kind of spontaneous planning should be a feature of all nursery and reception class planning.

Supporting the reception team

The head teachers were given the following advice to support their reception teams:

- Ensure that teachers and teaching assistants (TAs) have enough time to develop Early Years specialist expertise – not everyone is suited to working with this age group, or with the different approach to learning and teaching, and constant changes to the staff team will have a negative effect on quality. If a teacher is to be moved from Key Stage 1 or 2 into Early Years, they should have training opportunities the year before they move.
- Ensure the reception class has a consistent team of teacher and TA – so that children can develop trusting relationships and so that adults can develop shared consistent understandings. They need staff meeting and planning time together and TAs should be paid for this time. Remember, the TA can account for 50 per cent of teaching quality in EYFS.
- Ensure that all members of the SMT (Senior Management Team) are skilled and able to monitor and evaluate the quality of the learning environment and of children initiating their own learning (both in the classroom and outside). Use pages 6 and 7 of *Development Matters* as a guide to what you can expect to see children doing and how the environment and adults could be supporting them.
- Monitor the use of time in reception – children need uninterrupted time to work in depth (both independently and with an adult) and time out of the reception class should be kept to a minimum.

The session finished with a reminder of the importance of the Early Years in promoting positive attitudes to learning. If children lose their confidence and are switched off from learning at this early stage they will not flourish in Key Stage 1 and 2.

> for the mind is not a vessel that needs filling, but wood that needs igniting.
>
> Plutarch 50–120 AD

> Early years educators play a critical role in young children's learning. It is within their power to encourage feelings of fun and discovery in learning on the one hand or of dull drudgery on the other.
>
> Rumbold Report 1990 HMSO p. 36 par 4

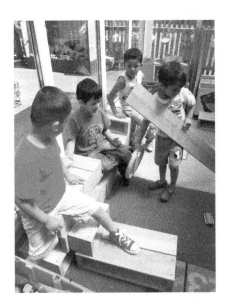

This group of boys is often engaged in adventurous and active role play. They explore the possibilities with the large blocks outdoors and collaborate to begin to build together.

As they build they adapt, change and then begin to formulate a plan of what they are going to build.

They decide to build a vehicle together – it's a tank.

They spend some time building the tank but then attention turns to planning their game, where they are going, what they plan to do and what they need.

The following day the boys return to the area talking about a plan they have already decided on – making the adventure playground – 'Palmer Park'. Talking, planning and working to make decisions together, they construct the first part of the 'adventure playground' and begin to balance and climb on parts of the equipment. They select the wooden blocks and also the tree blocks and branches to complete the different elements of the equipment.

They take turns to travel across and jump off the equipment, talking about who can jump farthest.

After some time, they stop climbing and talk about the left over blocks. Bilal and Ibrahim take the pieces left and make a 'see-saw' structure to accompany the climbing equipment.

What this reveals...

The group of boys work in collaboration very successfully. They plan together and share ideas. One boy initiated ideas in the first instance and this has served to support his peers develop their ideas in play too, over time as they work together over weeks. They are very interested in creating constructions together that support their role play narratives. They are very physically active in play and they are interested in active, adventurous role play narratives often involving fighting and rescuing others – 'saving the day'. They test out ideas and adapt plans as the play develops. New ideas evolve as they explore materials and their possibilities. This type of open-ended exploration of large construction is a successful vehicle to support their individual next steps in areas of learning; it also fully supports the development of the characteristics of effective learning. Moving forward the practitioners will use sensitive interventions and careful plans to develop more opportunities for these boys to develop their own individual next steps as a natural part of this play.

References

Early Years Foundation Stage Profile Handbook, 2014, Standards and Testing Agency.

Maclure, M. and Jones, L., *Becoming a Problem: How and Why Children Acquire a Reputation as 'Naughty' in the Earliest Years at School,* 2009, available at esrcsocietytoday.ac.uk.

Sykes, Elizabeth D. A., Bell. J. F., and Rodeiro, C. V., *Birthdate Effects a Review of the Literature from 1990 on,* 2009, Cambridge Educational Press.

For more information about the EYFS Profile and exemplification material see www.foundationyears.org.uk.

7 Case studies

This chapter contains case studies from practitioners that took part in the project. The studies have been collected from a variety of settings, from a pack away pre-school to reception classes. Each practitioner has described the impact of the project on their practice, peers and provision. Each one gives an insight into overcoming potential barriers and difficulties practitioners may face when developing effective observation, assessment and planning systems.

Impact on observational assessment in a Reception class

Sadie

My expectation for the course was to refine and consolidate my observation planning and assessment skills. I wanted to ensure that I was collecting quality information through rigorous observations of children's play and interactions. I wanted to support and guide my teaching assistants in their collection of observations and I was keen to find out how others used their observations to inform their planning on a daily basis.

As a result of the course I altered observation forms to include the age of the child. Found this really useful when relating the observation to the new curriculum and when considering what is expected of a child of that age when relating to child development guidelines.

I introduced focused children for the week – this initially helped me and my teaching assistant focus our attention and ensure that everyone was observed over the course of the term. However, after trialling this method, I found that I did less 'spontaneous observations' of 'wow' moments. We then needed to readdress the balance between focused and incidental!

My TA and I reflected on how to make quality observations and what constitutes *useful* information to collect. This is an ongoing process and observations are discussed daily.

Time to reflect and talk with my TA is invaluable! Together we can create a clear picture about how our children are developing and where they need to go next.

Impact on developing skills of the whole EYFS team in a school

Carrie – EYFS lead teacher

Our school is an Infant School in Farnborough. We have two form entry.

In class there are 26 children and our learning support assistants change every term. The class have formed a good bond and will look out for each other.

We wanted to develop our observation skills and have a solid training programme for learning support assistants who changed regularly, some of which had no experience in Reception. We also wanted to develop our ability to involve parents with observations at home.

As a result of the project we made more time to interact with and observe children, during child-initiated learning, rather than us leading activities. We were tending to value adult-led activities where we had our heads down and then missed the opportunities to observe the children demonstrating the skills they had learnt, through their own learning. It was only when we took time to do this that we realised the value of the child-initiated learning and how much we learnt about different children. We always used to plan time with other adult-led activities and now purposely plan sessions where we interact and observe.

We introduced the use of a focused observation for 5 minutes on a child and attempted to conduct one per child, per term. We found this really useful for all children as you gained so much information in that short period of time. It also informed you greatly about communication and language areas and PSED, which we were struggling to observe. This type of observation also had a huge impact upon us getting to really know and understand those 'quiet' children in the class that could just 'slip under the radar' because they just get on! You really gained a good insight into these children and it helped to plan next steps. The quality of our observations improved greatly. We realised that we were guilty of making judgements with our observations and whilst time constraints might make us still do that occasionally, when we are observing children, we are careful to make our observations factual about what the children do and say.

We also become more aware that we didn't always need to record a next step for an observation as it doesn't always lend itself to a next step. We involved other colleagues by holding a training session for all Early Years practitioners. We have also made videos, using iPads and use these for training on making observations. The whole team looks at observations together to moderate them and talk about their worth. We are also developing the use of our 4 teaching areas, to enable us to be able to pair up so teachers can model making observations for LSAs when they first come into the area.

We are developing 'wow' moment sheets to send home with parents for them to complete and return to us. We are anticipating that some parents might not be able to complete these so we have talked about running a short workshop before the end of school on a day, enabling parents to talk to you about their child and complete it. As we have outcomes for projects, having these available when they are in for an outcome would enable parents to fill it in at that point, with regards to each project too.

With our planning systems, we do now plan in more time to observe the children during child-initiated learning. We are more careful to plan for opportunities and so have more resources to hand, allowing children to show prior learning in their own situations. We are beginning to develop sheets to go up in areas such as the role play area, construction area etc., which suggest things to observe, resources to have readily available, questions to ask. We use our observations to plan for next steps for children or groups of children. At the start of projects, children are asked about what they already know and then we use their ideas to structure the project.

We feel through a result of the changes we have made, we are making more valued observations that provide us with a whole picture of the children. We have shared our changes through a staff meeting with the whole school and asked them to have a go at making an observation using our videos, which was very successful. We looked at the observations we make and assessments, as well as our tracking for children.

We still have a long way to go with all the changes as we have found we can only put some things in to place initially, in order for us to be successful. Therefore we will introduce even more new things after giving time to fully implement previous changes.

Impact on leading and managing change in practice in a pre-school

Sue – manager

We are a Pre-School in shared Church Hall premises, having to pack away occasionally. Ages of children range from 2 years to 4. We serve an area that has some social deprivation.

Sue took on the project so that:

Junior and inexperienced staff could be helped to develop and improve their OAP skills when managing the learning and education of key children.

From doing the course I, as a Manager, changed my attitude from one of despair and of blaming people for being unable to grasp in what was my opinion a fundamental skill. I had given up expecting staff could develop their skills as although I had given a lot of time to them in demonstrating and actually doing planning with them, very little improvement took place. The worst thing was that the planning I was doing was ignored too, which meant the Deputy Manager and I were planning for 50+ children between us by the end of the school year and it was really just for my own benefit!

The course has changed all that. Through having the opportunity to reflect, listen to Margaret's teachings and compare practice with others attending the course I became more patient. The key to change, was when Margaret challenged us to identify what we know about a child and write it down under the 7 areas of the EYFS. We, on the course, used written accounts of a child as an exercise and it made things a lot simpler. So I thought surely if staff knew a child well in having daily contact with them, they should be able to do the same and they could! We changed the form from the RDS to the progress sheet, using the example that Margaret gave us, following pages, photos, observations and evidence collected were looked at that had pointers for future development and were actually used when the progress of a child was being identified and recorded. The result is that all staff are now actively developing their skills.

We have also made a list of key phrases that staff can use so they are being more precise, e.g. using phrases like – 'J is demonstrating', 'has achieved', 'has the ability to...', 'shows interest in', 'with support is able to...' and this has worked well in that they do not write 'fuzzy', meaningless comments – such as 'J has a nice smile'!

As I changed my thinking, there were no issues – everyone grasped what was introduced to them hungrily and confidence has consequently risen in everyone.

Staff started to bring in their own ideas about presentation. We had previously made the learning journals ourselves out of card covered with coloured wallpaper. At a little expense we have used the suggestion of staff to buy presentation folders. All the learning journals look good and the content is also improving as staff are more interested in what they are doing.

The children also feel the same. They are eager to help stick in photos of what they are doing, initiate photos being taken of their achievements and they talk about what they have done in the past, whether they would like to repeat an activity for example.

We have:

Introduced different recording forms, given training on the wording and presentation of details needed whilst making observations and in planning. We have developed the cycle of OAP and have done this in bite sized chunks. For example, we are currently working on planning – teaching staff to look at observations, photos and the learning needs of the children recorded, in order to think what to include in future learning needs of the children they are Key Person to.

We have always met with parents to discuss their child's progress every term but not really involved them with planning. We now encourage parents to look at their child's learning journal before the progress review meeting and feedback we have been given by parents is positive and many make contributions in the planning now. We are incorporating parents' thoughts on the 'parent's view' part of the planning form, again, something we have not thought about doing in a formal way before.

Sue's pro formas appear on pages 77–79.

Impact on OFSTED outcomes in a pack away pre-school

Mena – manager

The pre-school is a 'pack-away' setting in a church hall. They have 38 children on roll and 9 members of staff. The setting is based in Farnborough and it has good links to its main feeder school. The setting had been involved in the ECaT project in Rushmoor. The manager had recently become supernumerary to the ratio for two sessions a week.

Why we did it

- The setting had had two satisfactory grades from OFSTED.

Their action was 'develop further observation and assessment systems to identify children's next steps across all areas of learning and to link into children's learning and development journeys.'

- The *improvement support programme* (support from the Early Years team) had helped identify the environment and observation, assessment and planning as areas for development.

Example of Sue's progress review

Prime areas – personal, social and emotional development

Self-confidence and self-awareness, managing feelings and behaviour, making relationships:

H has settled back into Pre-School brilliantly. She comes for 15 hours a week, Monday – Friday.

Her confidence has grown and she is steadily making friends with the other children and interacting with the adults. She really enjoys coming into the Pre-School environment and we are now able to identify her needs and interests.

H has recently started a PATHS group, which will help to distinguish her feelings and how she can manage and express them. In large groups, H needs encouragement to join in with discussion time and to express her ideas and views. She is much more confident in small groups and one to one.

Physical development

Moving and handling, health and self-care:

H is developing her fine motor skills and she uses scissors with great confidence. She needs a little correction to hold a pencil in the correct way but with more practice she will soon be able to achieve it. She is able to write her name and to achieve quite detailed drawings.

H enjoys doing PE and is very capable with her gross motor skills when moving over apparatus. She particularly enjoys the obstacle courses that we have set out in the past and we extend this to the other areas of learning, e.g. counting, by getting her to do various activities like a certain number of star jumps before going onto the next obstacle.

H is starting to understand the need to wash hands after using the toilet, before snacks and cooking activities.

Communication and language

Listening and attention, understanding, speaking:

As H has got to know the other children and staff she has developed her conversation skills and she enjoys telling us about things that happen at home. She can express her own ideas and views in self chosen activities such as in the role play area.

H now has the ability to do more than two things at once and will join in with the nursery rhymes she knows that use actions with great joy.

Specific areas – literacy

Reading and writing:

H spends a great deal of time in the book corner reading/looking at books or playing with the story sacks, where she has the great ability to make up her own stories.

She is able to write her name and engages in drawings where her mark making always has meaning. She also has been enthusiastic to make marks and patterns in dry materials such as coloured sand and flour and wet gloops.

Mathematics

Numbers, shape, space and measures:
H can count by rote to 10 and beyond. She can recognise numbers with confidence to 5 and beyond to 10 with a little prompting. She can order numbers in sequence independently.

H is able to identify and name shapes and can distinguish between big/little and talk about small, medium and large.

H likes to thread beads and is able to make a simple 1-1 repeating colour pattern using beads. She is able to talk and recognise position, talking about corners, edges, middle, top and bottom for example.

Understanding the world

People and communities, the world, technology:
We continue to be involved in outdoor activities and in particular walks in the local environment. H is able to recognise familiar walks and anticipate landmarks along a route. We set challenges when we are out, talking about sign posts, road names, looking at numbers on house doors or car number plates.

H has been involved in celebrations, learning about the customs and traditions of festivals and how they are celebrated. We will continue this learning throughout the spring term with all the festivals that occur at this time leading up to Easter.

In cooking activities she is learning about equipment and technology. We have talked about how ice has formed and snow during the recent snow that we had and H is confident and understands that the weather has to be very cold before ice is formed and can say what happens when ice is in warm conditions.

Expressive arts and design

Exploring and using media and materials, being imaginative:
H enjoys all aspects of painting and drawing and she has good scissor skills. She particularly enjoys making collages with various materials that we have at the drawing and writing table and she showed good thinking about where she wanted to place certain shapes.

H really enjoyed the paint mixing activity that we have done this term and she showed good knowledge of what colours she would get when mixing the primary colours together and she was very pleased with the beautiful rainbow that she painted too!

H still loves to play dress up in the role play area and at every opportunity when we have the chance for the children to dress up when they come into school, especially Halloween!

H uses her imagination in all of the arts. She is particularly strong in using her imagination in small world play and will spend a long time playing with figures and dolls at a dolls' house for example, but also making up stories with using figures and props in story sacks. She will use all available resources in her story making.

Example of an individual plan

List the child's interests:
Role-play area, small world play.
Reading: Books and using story sacks.

List the main strengths:
Using her imagination in a variety of ways.
Re-telling stories previously heard before using the various small figures and story sacks.

Review of progress – (main areas)
As H's confidence has continued to develop she has made friends with the other children. She has really good imagination that she uses in a variety of different situations.
She has developed her scissor skills and is getting very confident when using them.
H has made good progress in mathematical skills this term and she is getting confident particularly in her number recognition skills.

How would you like the child to develop?
1 Extend her interest in small world play and use it to encourage her to interact with other children.
2 Writing her name and practising fine motor skills she has made progress in so far e.g. scissor skills.
3 Gain skills in recognising emotions and to have the ability to communicate how she feels and how others are feeling too.
4 Encourage more use of the computer.

How will you achieve this?
1 Set up small world play activities with smaller groups in the CS room to encourage confidence building when interacting and sharing ideas with others.
2 Give H support and encouragement in various activities that include drawing, painting, mark making so that she develops the strength in her fingers.
3 H has joined a PATHS group that helps to develop emotional literacy.
4 Give H more opportunity and encouragement to have time at the computer and give one-to-one support.

Parents' views:

The setting manager was committed to improving quality practice.

What we did as a result of the training:

- Mena said she made many developments as a result of the training, but her main areas were the development of the environment and the development of their learning journals.
- In the training Mena recalled that Margaret said, '*You know how annoying it is when you go to Tesco's and they have had a change around and it takes ages to find the milk? Imagine what it's like for a child coming into your setting and it's different every day!*'

This inspired Mena to work with staff to develop a room layout. Then they developed continuous provision plans so everyone knew what to get out and why! The environment was then just regularly reviewed to check all the areas were working well and staff enhanced the areas based on their plans.

The OAP project inspired Mena to focus on the importance of child development knowledge. So she invested in Mary Sheridan's Child Development books and the whole staff began to use the developmental stages in their learning journals. The journals developed considerably over the course of the project. Mena led staff to have weekly time to keep journals updated, which then meant they were current and available everyday for parents to look at or take home. This then increased parents' notes in the journals too. The journals were now used as a 'lively' working document and this had the result of helping parents develop relationships with the Key Person. Previously parents had spoken to the manager to share information or news – now they go to the Key Person. The now effective learning journals feed into the individual plans for the children; this in turn informs the enhancements for the environment.

The impact of the project:

- The changes to the environment – having continuous provision in static areas – had the immediate effect of calming the children down. They played for longer in the areas of play. Staff knew where everything should go in the room, so time could be spent just adding any extra enhancements based on plans. The continuous provision plans enabled staff to consider and discuss what learning might go on in that area as well as knowing what should be there!
- The changes to the learning journals have made the planning more effective because it is based on the children's next steps. Also, raising the profile of the learning journal to make it a real working document, updated and shared regularly, has strengthened the role of the Key Person in the setting. The relationships between parents and the Key Persons are more effective – parents don't feel they need to go to the manager first. Parents have a voice in the learning journal, and staff are confident to now be pro-active with this. If they feel a parent has not reviewed the journal in a while, they might encourage them to take it home overnight to share with their partner.
- The setting had another OFSTED inspection after the project ended. The manager was delighted that they achieved a 'Good' after two satisfactory OFSTED grades.

The current OFSTED report states:

> Children take pleasure in their learning and achieve well in relation to their starting points. This is because they have good opportunities to choose their play materials and follow their individual learning styles. Observations are regularly completed and recorded together with photographs of activities that

are kept for each child in their own 'Learning Journal'. Staff evaluate their observations to identify learning priorities for each child. The children's records clearly show the good progress each child makes and how their next steps are identified and planned for. The educational programme ensures the children are offered interesting and challenging experiences across the seven areas of learning.

And:

An excellent partnership with parents ensures children's individual needs are met. They complete an 'All about me' sheet when the child starts at the setting describing children's needs, abilities, likes and dislikes. This helps staff to value each child as an individual. Parents are kept well informed about their child's care and progress. They are encouraged to contribute to their children's Learning Journals and are encouraged to share children's progress in their learning and development made at home.

Impact on the role of the lead practitioner and the development of quality practice in a pre-school setting that had undergone change

Natalie

Natalie started the project just after the Pre-School had gone through a number of changes. The setting had moved to a brand new building that was twice the size of the last room the Pre-School had been based in for 25 years. The number of children had risen from 24 children per session to now being able to have 40 children per session, so they had over 90 children on roll. There was now a large staff group, some of whom worked part time.

At the start of the project we were trying to cope with all the changes we had been through. We suddenly had lots more children and more staff. Our initial concern was our planning. We had some long term planning available but we were struggling with our short term plans. We didn't have a system in place and so we were asked if we wanted to join the project.

Now we do have a system that is working for us. We have a group of focus children that we observe, assess and then plan for. My role continues as a lead practitioner and I oversee the OAP in our setting. So I look at the progress reviews that are carried out and the individual plans and I bring the plans together as the starting point for our plans.

Our planning changed a lot. We needed to start somewhere with planning as this was a real concern, so we looked at what other people did in the first place. We started with our plans being a reflective journal where we wrote down what we had done that session. During the project we focused on observational assessment and then looked at what planning should contain. At first I led the others on the team to look at what we could add to our plans and encouraged everyone to contribute to them.

As we reflected on our plans and with advice, we wanted to make sure that we recorded the adult planned activities too. So we adapted the planning to show what adults have planned from our assessments and also to write down what the children do in their child-initiated play. We stuck to the journal style of planning and we put in photos and observations from all staff. This took a while to get in to place and I have worked with the deputy to ensure that everyone remembers to write down relevant things in to the journal.

On the project I found that what worked for me was to listen and talk about my situation with Margaret and the others, and then to adapt ideas to suit my setting. My setting was the only one that was so big with so many children and staff so we had our own difficulties to overcome. Finding time to meet regularly to discuss the children was hard; in fact we couldn't do it. So we adapted things to make it work for us. So the Key Person could meet with me or the deputy to talk about the children for assessment and planning. Also, by being given time to look through the progress reviews and individual plans I was then able to discuss issues with members of staff on an individual basis. We also couldn't get all members of staff to observe all focus children. So the Key Person would lead the observations on the child and be supported by me and the deputy.

To make sure everyone knows about next steps and planning going forward, we now use one of the whiteboards to act as a reminder so everyone can easily see what things are being planned and who for.

We have made so many changes since the start of the project. We did start by often putting out all activities for the children, but now we have new storage furniture and can offer continuous provision for child-initiated learning. We carry out regular progress reviews, at least once a term and these are clearly linked to the plans we make for children. We share reviews with parents too so they know all about how they are progressing and their next steps.

I was able to support staff and talk about good practice in staff meetings. Also, as I worked alongside them in the room, I could say things like – 'that's really good don't forget to write that in the plans' or staff would come to me to say 'Is this the sort of thing I should write?' I could use the tasks we used in the training, back with the others to talk about issues we had.

The project started with observations and so I used the examples of good and bad observations to take back to look at with staff. We looked at how useful our observations were and thought about what makes a good observation. We started off by using the paperwork given to us on the course for focused observations, progress review and individual plans. We have gone on to change most of these and adapted things to suit us.

We really know the children well and know what their next steps are and what to do to plan for the children. During our last inspection, which was about five months ago, the inspector spoke to me for a long time about the OAP systems in our setting. I was confident that I knew and could talk about what we did and why. I also thought that all members of staff would know too if they were asked.

Some quotes from Natalie's last OFSTED, graded GOOD (2):

Teaching is good as staff provide a wide range of play opportunities and focus strongly on enabling children to learn through following their interests.

The staff have a good understanding of each child's individual needs and stage of development. Consequently, they effectively plan and support children to make good individual progress in all areas of learning.

Staff have high expectations for their key children and plan relevant and challenging next steps for their learning. As children start at the pre-school a range of information is used to develop an understanding of their development. Staff support this through home visits before the children start. Each child has a next steps plan and staff also use a notice board to identify key objectives for each child throughout the pre-school. This ensures every member of staff can effectively support each child's learning not just the Key Person.

The impact on consistent practice in a Nursery class in a primary school

Lisa – teacher in a Nursery class of a primary school

For our class the project had a huge impact on *consistent practice*. The approaches suggested in the project enabled us to put a system in place that not only ensured that we focus very clearly on every child as an individual – but we all discuss them regularly as a whole team. We were then able to ensure that we knew we could plan together for each child but also have a shared understanding of every child's learning and development. Without this we couldn't make the most of all the spontaneous planning that goes on as we observe or get involved in the children's play. We now all know what the children need as well as what they are interested in. This lets us make the most of those spontaneous planning opportunities that are so rich and effective because they are rooted in the child's initiated play.

So for example, it can be quite straightforward to observe what the child is interested in and so we can extend this by offering more resources or provision. So we might generally know what the child likes to do. But if we also know they would benefit from developing their fine motor skills further then the resources we provide could extend that interest *and* also support fine motor development too. So those whole team conversations we developed as part of our focus child system allowed us to be more *effective* and to be more *consistent* in our approach – everyone had a good knowledge of each child.

What we did – the focus child system:

Sometimes in the school, as teachers we have taken on the role of leading on assessment and planning, then sharing information with other staff. This was due to expectations, working hours of support staff and time in general! Our new approach enabled the assessment and planning to be more of a dialogue between all staff also sharing our observations, ideas and knowledge.

In our class we have always carried out 'long' observations (Margaret calls them 'focused observations') as well as short observations, annotated photographs and work samples. However, we found that for some children we had lots of evidence and others we had less (probably not enough for our purposes). So we wanted to put a *focus child system* in place to ensure every child was focused on closely by all staff each term as suggested in the project. We decided to select three children per session, per week to focus on – they would be our 'focus' children.

All staff would observe all of those children during the week. Initial barriers were that we found that at a time we wanted to observe for a five minute observation on a child, someone else was already doing it!

Then we found that we had all carried out observations on the same child in the same day – not ideal as we wanted a breadth of the child's experience to consider.

So we devised a table. The teacher I job-share with drew up a grid that told us which child would be observed by which practitioner, on which day – then we would have a picture of the child through the week in a variety of contexts. So during one session we would each be given a different child to observe – but over the course of a week we would all have observed each child.

The grid is something like the diagram below but it shows the whole term rather than just one week. The three focus children are Sam, Joe and Anne. Sara and Lisa job-share, Jo and Hannah are both full time practitioners:

Practitioner	Monday	Tuesday	Wednesday	Thursday	Friday
Sara/Lisa	Sam	Anne		Joe	
Jo	Joe	Sam		Anne	
Hannah	Anne	Joe		Sam	

To organise the focused observations we had an informal discussion and agreement about the sort of time we would carry out the observations so that we weren't all observing for the same five minutes! For example, the nursery nurse would say 'I'll observe Sam sometime in the first hour of the session', the nursery assistant would take the second hour to do a five minute observation of Joe and then I could observe Anne at some point in the last hour of the session. This worked for us although it might seem a bit contrived, but we needed a way to get a system established in the early days. Things are more fluid now as it is so well established.

As we continued the system we had to review and discuss how things were running. We noted that sometimes it was difficult to maintain complete focus on that child for five minutes as other children approached us to play or interact. As a result we decided that the other two members of staff, where possible, would try to ensure they would be available to help and support any children approaching the observer during the five minute observation time – although this wasn't always possible as you can imagine! We thought about the five minute observation more flexibly. If possible we would continue to observe even if interrupted and compile notes afterwards if it wasn't possible to note things at the time – we found we could retain information quite well. We were aware of not needing 'prolonged breaks' from interaction to observe. So we stuck to five minutes only, even if it was tempting to observe for longer. We decided we could observe some play quite well whilst still needing to be involved with other children.

With the focused observations completed for the week, we met to read through the observations and other short observations made, along with their learning journals. We had to make the most of time around the session and PPA time. We discussed everything we knew about the children and then completed the *individual planner* with a *review of their progress*. Together we decided on appropriate next steps and what we could plan to provide for these. It was really useful to think of other children that would also benefit from those planned experiences or enhancements. We always made sure that the next steps were planned with the children's interests and fascinations in mind. Due to time available to talk together, the teachers wrote up the individual plans and reviews more formally after the team discussions, when we just captured notes.

The following week's plans would include some detail of those planned experiences and enhancements with children's names next to them as a reminder to us. Of course we wouldn't make children play with the enhancements or planned experiences but we hoped that by carefully linking them to their interests and strengths too they would be drawn to them naturally. We also found that of course some adult involvement to support those experiences would make them irresistible! So there would be a good mix of child-initiated, adult-initiated and adult-led experiences all working together to support children develop their next steps. We then moved on to focus on the next group of children.

What we did – planning and parents

Our planning has changed lots of times. Currently we complete daily plans. Part of the planning is typed in advance (the night before) and there is also room for annotation and spontaneous plans to be recorded. Sometimes we change the planned experience and then just cross it out and write in what happens instead and why. We always make sure that the learning intention is clearly recorded so we don't just have the experiences written down, that ensures everyone knows the intended outcome even if other outcomes emerge too. That includes visitors and parents too. When our head teacher pops in to do her learning walk, she is able to look at the daily plan to see at a glance what is planned and why.

Working with parents added a new dimension to how we wrote our individual plans and next steps for the children. Being very guilty of 'teacher talk' we thought we need to write in a clearer, more parent friendly way and make sure that we had thought about possibilities for what parents might do at home to support next steps. We wanted to make sure these were doable! And fun. We had to think about what families would naturally be doing – we know that families are so busy outside of school time we didn't want them to think they had to do something extra! We wanted to help our parents think about what they already do and the value of it or what they already do and could perhaps 'enhance' based on the children's next steps. When we have our termly meetings with parents we use the child planners as part of the conversation and fill in the next steps together. That allows us to talk about what the child loves to do at home and beyond (where many of them have very rich experiences that can't be offered easily in school) and strengthen what we know and can do, as well as provide support for what parents can do too.

We introduced a home school book that goes home on a Friday. We usually put in a brief note about what we have done this week and plans or ideas for next week. We offer a simple idea to support home learning – having a listening walk on the way to the park, maybe a simple play-dough recipe with dough gym ideas or suggested books we have looked at or might be looking at. Parents are encouraged to note anything they want to in the book. Some add photos if they went somewhere at the weekend. Some just add notes 'Hannah loved Pirate Day – she's been making eye patches and maps all weekend!' We have found it invaluable. It has strengthened our view and knowledge of the whole child. The books have been very well received by parents. The impact on the children has also been good, as they love their books and often when they bring them in they go to the book corner straight away to share it with a member of staff and their friends. Children love photos of themselves and their families and it has really supported language and PSED in particular, as well as their motivations and play within the class.

Moving on – capturing the child's voice

Since the project we have developed the focus child system further in the light of another training session I went on. On the days we are not carrying out the five minute observations we decided to try a new way to capture the 'child's voice' for those focus children. We take photos of the focus children at regular intervals during that day. We then print them out with the child – if our computer allows, if not we look at them on the computer or camera – and we scribe what they say about what they were doing. If we can print them there and then the children can cut out and stick their selected photos (usually all of them!) and we write the child's own comments alongside the photos. We try to get them to think about what they really loved about a certain experience, perhaps the process or what made it so good. This is then added to their learning journal. So this allows children to reflect on their achievements and supports the very informal discussion around learning between the teacher and child.

Our learning journals have been reviewed too. We add the focused observations to the learning journals and the child's voice photos. We have continued to capture short observations and photos too. However, we are careful about what we include – everything included must be useful and meaningful. We agreed that we really value the use of photographs in our learning journals. The photos create a picture of the child more accessibly and quickly than other methods. When we are busy we can take a photo or series of photos and annotate after the session. Some trainers I have heard think photos are over used, they may well be. We agreed that we believe that our photos are useful to us, we are all experienced in Early Years and we don't take meaningless photos of children just smiling at the camera! All our photos reveal something about the child and all together capture the essence of the experience, strengths, interests, learning styles and progress made over time. It also enables the journal to be shared easily with the child to look at how they have progressed and developed over time. We want to make sure we work effectively. We want to make sure that we capture the evidence we need in the most efficient way possible – our time is precious and we use it well. We only take and print photos we need to capture the learning that is taking place. We have found that this is the quickest and most effective way for us to manage our observational assessments but we have a system in place.

This is what we do. We all have cameras that we carry around with us. Each camera can also video. We have a laptop set up to an interactive whiteboard throughout the session. We set up a folder with today's date on the laptop's desktop. We take any photos we want to during the session and then plug in the cameras and download the photos to the folder that is ready. We then have the photos displayed as a slideshow on our whiteboard as the parents come in to collect the children at the end of the session. The parents can see what happened today, children are keen to show parents photos of them at play. At the end of the session we send photos to the printer – usually wallet size prints. We match them to observations we made or annotate them as needed. This works for us and might not work for other people.

To summarise, we believe the impact for us has been:

- Greater shared knowledge of the children as individuals
- Greater shared knowledge of the children's strengths, interests and next steps
- Closer links with parents
- More information about the children's learning within the setting for parents
- More opportunity for parents to have a voice and be consulted
- More impact on home learning
- Consistent practice
- Greater recognition of the role and capabilities of support staff
- More effective spontaneous planning
- Direct and clear links between the assessments and the planning

We will continue to look critically at what we do to ensure we are doing the best we can for all of our children. The project has encouraged us to review, reflect and re-evaluate; this won't stop just because the project has. We have a stable staff group but as people may leave in the future we have tools that we can use to support new staff and we have a clear system in place which ensures that we all work together and share our knowledge and expertise. We are all still learning too – even after all these years!

We had our latest OFSTED school inspection two months ago as I write this. The inspectors didn't really look closely at our planning or our learning journals. They did talk to us about the starting points of the children and progress. For our class, they did spend most of their time observing practice in all contexts. They observed adult planned and led groups and child-initi-ated experiences. They spoke to children and observed. We had three visits during the two days. They gathered the majority of their evidence about prac-tice in our class through observation.

The report stated:

> Children join the school in the nursery with skills and knowledge which are typical for their age, although higher proportions than usual speak English as an additional language. The excellent resources and teaching mean they make a rapid start to their learn-ing in the nursery.

and

> Teaching in the nursery is outstanding.

We feel that the project with the practical ideas that support the principles and training materials have helped us to strengthen our consistent practice.

Top tips that helped us:

- Involve everyone in assessment and planning
- Share knowledge and expertise
- Put manageable and workable systems in place – this can take some discussion, organisation and review to get them right for you
- Focused observations can give real insight and challenge what you think you know about a child
- Keep reflecting

Planning example

This is an example of our daily planning that we use at the moment. We have tried weekly planning but we have found this was so subject to change (as we follow children's interests and build on them as a vehicle for learning) that we decided to go back to daily planning. We started off handwriting the plans but senior leaders in the school preferred to have the planning typed up – so we begin the day with some parts of the plan typed in but we leave sections blank to complete during the day and annotated as we go:

Planned experiences:

3D reclaimed materials, collage materials, paint, etc for model making/ playdough (creative workshop)-
Use story stimulus as possible starting point to encourage engagement and creative ideas. Own selection of tools - encourage use of one handed tools to develop fine motor skills and gross motor strength. Possible ideas, maps, eye patches, telescopes, boats, flags etc. Playdough islands, TS treasure island
(PD, L, PSED- independence, fine motor control, gross motor strength, use of tools and following recipe) EAD – using imagination to create own products and find own ways and preferences' to express ideas.
GM - create photos for visual timetable, four experiences represented for intensive support.

Snack time: HS – talking point (CL): what did Pirate Peg say?

Enhancements based on
observations/interests/next steps:
Interests observed last week – pirates, pirate songs, building, in role creative play, transporting, storytelling, parties and celebrations, journeys

CL/EAD/PD - **creative construction**, large blocks, sheets, crates, planks – ships?
PD – **mark making on the move** outdoors – opportunities, painting with water on easel, maps, chalks on the ground
CL – **story area** – cloakroom- offered with adult to share stories and music, pirate songs
PSED – **indoor block play**, ensure this is enhanced before session starts to promote engagement on entry (from obs) - working together to complete, negotiation and turn taking, sharing ideas. Small world figures/pirates

---

**Learning priorities / next steps /
planning brought forward / other notes**

Next steps:

CL-Speaking – develop confidence and opportunities, recasting, modelling and match plus one (identified cohort) small group **support in CI play**

PSED – MR – **adult involvement in CI play**, spontaneous small groups, storytelling, in role play.

PD – MH – **mark making** all around, large motor opps, arm, shoulder, core strength development in outdoors in particular (**building, transporting, climbing**).

L – **storytelling**, mark making and early writing, teacher scribing to model, some letter formation (LB, HJ, HT, PK, GO)

M – Number/counting/numerals – **register**, how many children, link to numerals. Order to five – **pirate clues**.

Monday 18th Nov

Spontaneous play/observations

Adult led group time
L.O - develop interest and enjoyment of in role storytelling, adding ideas and suggestions to a narrative (CL,L)
-Sustain attention and listening (CL)
-recall other stories/narratives from previous experience and use to inform ideas (CL,L)
- making links in learning, links with real life events
-Consider purpose of writing, adult modeling to support composition as a group (CL,L)

In role storytelling – "Pirate Peg"
A message in a bottle - any clues? Read message – dilemma what shall we do? Help to buid a ship? Pirate crew? Clues to find Pirate Peg's map. Send a reply, compose together. Plan what to do.Two groups share planning ideas teacher scribes and children encouraged to add own drawings and writing. (PD,L)
Use themes from story to enhance play themes – building and constructing, letter writing, flags, boats, telescopes, map making, emails, text, messages in a bottle etc.
HS – GM – promote engagement with picture book, naming objects, using makaton sign (CL)
JS – support planning group, promote talk and working together (CL, PSED).

Adult led group time
Story – The Night Pirates! **LS**
L.O – CL - sustain attentive listening, recall events, make a simple prediction about what might happen next, make a personal response to a text. Making Links to previous experiences, play.

Introduce book. Talk about "title" and "author" and "illustrator". Begin to share the story, what do you think will happen next? Anticipation. What has happened to the house? What do you think is going to happen next? What would you do?(CL)
Share a message from Pirate Peg on talking Peg, clues to what she looks like...
JS – support GM – own picture book.

Adult led group time
Learning Outcomes:

Description of experience (e.g. story)

Adult led group time
Learning Outcomes

Description of experience (e.g. music or songs etc)

Learning priorities / next steps /
planning brought forward / other notes

Monday

Spontaneous play/observations

Planned experiences:

Snack time:

**Enhancements based on
observations/interests/next steps:**
Interests observed last week – linked to AOL

Impact on the development of practice in a baby room of a day nursery

Kate Bradbury, Lead Practitioner – OAP journey

The YMCA Nursery in Gosport is a friendly community-based day nursery located within the grounds of a college. We offer care and a play-based curriculum for children aged 4 months to 5 years, in age appropriate rooms.

We wanted to see how our Observation, Assessment and Planning (OAP) compared to other settings and how we could improve on what we were doing. We were already in the process of developing our planning, so the OAP experience was something that was of significant interest to us.

One of the first changes we made was to the observation format (example 1 at the end of this section). The Development Matters section was taken out (these could sometimes be too broad, especially for the babies) and practitioners would often find the 'best fit'. It was replaced with Evidence of Significant Learning. Once the observation has been linked with the EYFS, the relevant area is circled and labelled with the appropriate age band. Each age band is highlighted with a different colour and this information is then transferred onto the individual child's Tracking Sheet. The 7 areas of the EYFS are broken down further into the sub sections (e.g. an observation can be linked to PSED, making relationships). This area is now quicker to fill in and is more streamlined and factual. This allows the Key Person to see the progress the child is making and in which areas they have strengths and which they need support in. Some observations do not necessarily match the statements in the EYFS. Characteristics of Effective Learning sometimes fit better, so we use these too. After all, we should be focusing on the Unique Child and they do not fit into a book!

We added a learning context section to give a better background to the observation (where the child is and whether the activity is child-initiated, adult-initiated or adult-supported).

The next step section was taken out of each type of observation as practitioners felt that because the box was there, they needed to have a next step. This is not always necessary, sometimes enhancements, adult modelling or consolidation of an activity is appropriate. If we feel we need to write a 'next step' it is written on the 'What's next?' form, which is placed in the child's Learning Journey. The learning that we would like to take place is also written on the short-term planning.

We have short observations, used for quick jottings. We also use the longer extra evidence observations (A4 size) that follow the same format, which can be used for longer observations, such as observing an art activity or to include photographs. Focused observations are used for those children who we feel need to have some additional observation, for example, a new child, a child with a behavioural issue or those that tend to blend in.

As a result of the OAP training, we have introduced Learning Priorities (example 2). All children now have a Learning Priority (written in a clear and concise way), displayed on the room's Learning Priority Board for all to see. This allows all practitioners to know what each individual child's focus is and therefore support them to achieve it. The Learning Priority is also placed in the child's Learning Journey and is shared with parents.

For us, the thing that has changed the most has been the way we plan. It has taken many changes to get to where we are now. The most important thing about planning is that it is manageable, and focuses on the children's development and learning. In addition, the practitioners need to have confidence in it.

All our planning (indoor and outdoor activities) incorporates the 'YMCA Way', using the 6 values: listening, caring, welcoming, inspiring, exciting and active.

The Baby Room Planning has changed from an individual child's table format (Figure 3). We used this planning style initially, so the information would flow between observations and you could see the progression between experiences more clearly. This was teamed with a list of current activities to do/experiences to have (so all practitioners knew what each child was interested in). The idea worked initially but as time went on the staff felt it was too time consuming and as a result most were not using it effectively.

Now, we have introduced the PLOD (Possible Lines of Development) system, so we take an interest that some children are showing and go from there. It has been trialled for several months and it seems to be working well. Lots of observations are being written and displayed. Our most successful PLOD so far was about textures; it created a really full board and prompted the next interest, which was food. We have a tick chart to fill in, as we write an observation, so we know which children have been observed and how many times! There are several PLOD Boards on the go at any time, so the aim is that all children are being planned for. It is up to the Key Person to keep an eye on the board, to read the observations on the children and decide the 'what's next?' for them. This is then linked on the board and in their Learning Journeys, as it happens. Observations can also be linked to individual Learning Priorities if appropriate.

Everyone is happy with the changed planning system and it seems to be working, therefore effective. These boards are very visual and are changed frequently, as the interest comes to an end. Parents have taken an interest in the boards too and it has provided a start to some interesting conversations, strengthening our home-nursery link.

Once the PLOD Boards are completed, we take photos of them and file them away in the Children's Interest Folder. We also add additional evidence such as photos, children's work, and descriptions/evaluations of activities. Photocopies of all observations are added too (the originals go in the individual Learning Journeys).

We have just created a Characteristics of Effective Learning Board to display the observations that are not interest related and also for the younger babies (we felt that sometimes they were being missed out). Again, we have a tick chart and the Key Person has the same responsibilities as those for the PLOD Board.

Also on display are our 'We are learning to . . .' boards. These are for children who are at the same developmental stage. For example, we currently have 4 boards: a sitting aided/sitting unaided, a crawling, a walking and a feeding ourselves. These are very visual as they contain a photograph and name for each child, making it easy for practitioners/visitors to know instantly what developmental stage an individual child is at.

The Baby Room is just introducing small group planning activities taken from 'Babbling Babies – Activities to Build Babies' Language Development' by ICAN. We will plan weekly, using activities from the five different areas: learning to listen; learning and understanding new words; expressing myself; exploring and developing; playing and interacting. Activities can be adapted for children aged 0–6, 6–12, 12–18 months, so the individual needs of each child can be met. Activities will be repeated throughout the week, so consolidation of learning and experiences can take place.

The Toddler and Pre-School rooms use the PLOD style of planning too. Each having a weekly spontaneous planning board – that may focus on several current interests at a time, activities/enhancements that happen immediately as a reaction to an interest. They also have a medium-term planning PLOD – one that focuses on a current theme or interest such as spring.

In addition, to these boards, the older rooms have small group planning/key group time – together time for the toddlers and language and listening time for Pre-school.

Each room is working on their List of Entitlement. This is a list of areas of interest that capture the majority of children's imagination over the year. For example: spring (growing), summer (holidays/beach), autumn (exploring surroundings) and winter (Christmas). Trips to the local shops or places of interest may be placed on this list.

We have also now completed our update of the long-term planning. Mind maps were put up all around the nursery (in each room) for all practitioners to make a contribution to. A mind map for each area. This allowed everyone to feel they had an input and have some ownership over the long-term planning. From the mind maps, information was then transferred to a table format (Figure 4) and permanently displayed in the areas, along with a photograph.

We have learnt and grown so much on our journey so far and we will continue to do so. Our advice for those starting out on their journey would be to prioritise what you would like to change, focus on these elements first and other things can follow. Everything does not have to be implemented immediately, as the saying goes – 'Rome wasn't built in a day'. Also be aware that others may have not caught up with your thinking, people take time to get on board with your idea – the analogy of the leader being in the fast car (they have done the research and have seen the benefits) and the other members of your team getting on a bus, they all get on at different points but everyone arrives at the destination eventually, really made sense. Finally don't lose heart; it may take several changes before you find what works in your setting. It is important to have a system that everyone uses and understands.

Kate's forms appear on pages 93–95.

Impact for our local Early Years Advisory Team

The impact of this project for us, is that we have developed an effective **new model** for supporting settings by bringing together our bespoke training element, our improvement support programme and peer support principles.

Our training and support offers have complemented and enhanced one another; they have worked together to heighten each other's effect. By threading through training messages into our surgeries and visits, we have supported understanding of those messages. The training sessions have enhanced our support, as the trainer developed tasks and training to enable the practical implementation of areas we identified during our visits and work with settings.

We have found that rather than replicating our support work a number of times in several settings, this approach has enabled us to work more effectively and efficiently. We

This is the short observation format we are currently using. The extra evidence observation looks the same; it just fills the A4 sheet!

Observation

Name of child:	Key person:
Date:	Observed by:

Evidence of significant learning:

PSED   CL   PD   L   UW   M   EAD

Child-Initiated (CI)   Adult-Initiated (AI)   Adult Supported (AS)

Learning context (where the child is): Indoors/outdoors

Observation:

This is the Learning Priority table which we currently use, both on the Learning Priority Boards and in the children's individual Learning Journey.

Date	Learning Priority	Achieved

Date	Learning Priority	Achieved

Date	Learning Priority	Achieved

Date	Learning Priority	Achieved

Children's Individual Planning

Name:

Observation Date:	What learning would you like them to experience next?	Evaluation
Indoors/outdoors Schema?	Adult role/resources/enhancements	YMCA values? Listening Caring Welcoming Inspiring Exciting Active

Long-term planning for continuous provision of home corner

Key Learning Intentions and experiences

- Play alongside others (PSED:16–26 months)/Gradually able to engage in pretend play activity with other children (PSED:16–26 months)/Interested in others and starting to join in (PSED:22–36 months)/Can play in a group, extending and elaborating play ideas (PSED:30–50 months)
- Copies familiar expressions (CL:16–26 months)/Uses a variety of questions (CL:22–36 months)/Uses simple sentences (22–36 months)/Beginning to use word endings (CL:22–36 months)/Builds up vocabulary that reflects the breadth of their experiences (30–50 months)/Uses talk in pretending that objects stand for something else (CL:30–50 months)
- Dresses with help (PD:30–50 months)
- Enjoys filling and emptying containers (M:16–26 months)/ Begins to use the language of size (M:22–36 months)
- Uses some number names accurately in play (M:30–50 months)/Uses positional language (M:30–50 months)
- In pretend play, imitates everyday actions and events (UW:22–36 months)/Shows interest in different occupations and ways of life (UW:30–50 months)/Seeks to acquire basic skills in turning on and operating some ICT equipment (UW:22–36 months)/Shows an interest in technological toys (UW:30–50 months)
- Begin to make believe by pretending (EAD:22–36 months)/Uses available resources to create props (EAD:30/50 months)

Permanent resources

- Cooker, food, plates, bowls, cutlery, kitchen appliances, till, phone, menus, magazine rack, table and chairs, dressing up clothes, hair-dressers, babies and cot

Appropriate language

- What is your baby doing?
- What food are you cooking?
- Who do you want to dress up as today?
- Who is on the telephone?

Remember to use open-ended questions. Key words as permanent resources. Additional words may be used depending on what role play is happening.

Possible enhancements

- Real life objects/mark-making equipment
- Other resource boxes – vets, doctors, etc
- Open-ended materials – cardboard tubes, material

Resource organisation

- Clear boxes labelled correctly
- Open and accessible space
- Accessible resources
- Resources checked and damaged toys replaced

Role of the adult

- To support the children in play
- Play alongside/with the children
- Use appropriate vocabulary
- Model the children's play
- Give children ideas, move their interest on
- Develop the area into the current children's interest, pet shop, doctors, castle

could work with a number of our settings all in one day to explore the same issues. This freed up other times for us to support and develop other issues with settings.

We have repeated the initial project with the local schools and used a similar model for the delivery of a child development project. Other areas within Hampshire have also used this approach to develop OAP systems in their schools and settings.

Settings that we have supported over some time have made clear improvements; this has been seen in OFSTED reports as well as our own review of support. The lead practitioners – our 'Champions' – unanimously reported their growth in confidence and understanding of the OAP cycle. They also were strongly in favour of the approach we had taken to training; this enabled them to develop relationships, peer support, deeper understanding and to find a platform to share and resolve their issues and concerns. We have a common approach and shared understanding that is advocated by the whole team. The settings are secure with the terms and the processes introduced during the project, with a much clearer insight into terms such as 'next steps', 'child initiated' and 'continuous provision' – and what they **really** mean.

On reflection, our own 'project approach' mirrored the systematic approach to the OAP cycle as promoted in our training. As a team we came together to gather our observations of the practitioners and settings. We assessed their needs and considered their learning styles and the variety of resources and strategies we had available. We put together a plan for our project. As our plans and the project progressed, we reflected, assessed and reviewed to match the content to the needs and interests of our delegates. We altered plans to address the identified areas to be developed – the 'Learning Priorities'.

This 'project' model continues and as we continue to support the work of the OAP 'Champions' within their own settings, we also look to the future as their work will extend outwards to support other practitioners in other settings. The aim of which is to build practitioner confidence and peer support across the locality – making a difference for children in our settings. We strive to produce effective training and support and believe that this is implemented most effectively by a confident, well informed and dynamic Early Years' workforce. Our aim is that lead practitioners are well supported, equipped and resourced to lead, manage and **innovate** to ensure quality improvements are sustained.

During the review of training and support when we identified the common request for planning support, there were other possibilities available. One option – (perhaps quicker, cheaper but less effective!) – would have been to offer a blank pro forma for short-term planning and say 'Do it this way!' – we have been asked for this on previous occasions. However, we know the format of a plan, the layout, number of boxes etc., is not the route to real quality. Quality is found in the **content** of that plan and its roots in **excellent observation and assessment**. So instead of presenting a pre-packaged bundle of generic forms, we have facilitated opportunity for creativity, for imagination and for empowerment.

Through this project we have given each setting a 'toolkit' and the training to develop a skilled lead practitioner, to create their own work and to adapt and grow with experience. One size does not fit all with this approach. The deep understanding of the OAP cycle allows practitioners to make their own informed choices and to continue to develop and change as their experience and knowledge grows long after our project ended. This empowerment of practitioners who fully recognise their vital role, skills and their ability to innovate, can lead to raised levels of self esteem and pride in their work. The result being motivated, enthused and reinvigorated practitioners who know they can make a difference for every child.

Ultimately, our aim is to make Early Years' education exciting, engaging and truly effective for **every** child. Each child has a right to begin the world of education in a setting in which she or he will thrive and blossom. If we also offer a 'one size fits all' curriculum that requires the child to 'fit its mould' this can lead to failure and low levels of achievement. Therefore, we know that observation and assessment must be our starting points to planning effective provision.

When we start with the child, know and celebrate what the child can do, loves to do and then build on this, then we know we are doing the best for that child. If a child is fully engaged, motivated and supported by interested adults to take the next steps in the learning journey, what more can we do?

8   Tracking progress – a rough guide

After our OAP project, we delivered other projects in our locality. The first supported child development and another, most recently, was concerned with **tracking progress**. This was very much in response to the need for managers to have responsibility for and in-depth knowledge of the progress children are making in their settings. The project explored why tracking systems may be a useful tool, how to track and how to use data for quality improvement.

Thoughts on tracking

In the context of practitioners' **sound knowledge of child development** and **robust systems for observation, assessment and planning**, many settings use the summative assessments made to collate data to track the progress of all children. At regular intervals practitioners will make a 'progress review', which captures a picture of a child at that point in time. The review can reflect achievements across areas of learning and development, characteristics of effective learning the child displays, interests, strengths and ways forward (learning priorities).

Leaders and managers have a responsibility to ensure that high-quality provision within their settings is supporting and enabling children to make progress in their learning and development over time. Many leaders will know about the progress children are making through their close involvement with the practice within the setting, the children and their families. They will use all their knowledge of the evidence of learning through discussions with practitioners, review of recorded evidence and observation of the children, to collate information to create a clear picture of progress made. Through the use of tracking progress tools to compile a data set, managers can have a 'general overview' of how each child is progressing, how groups are making progress and also identify where individuals or cohorts are not progressing as expected.

The use of the data raises questions for managers and their staff – is this a concern, is this part of 'normal' development, have I spotted a trend with the language attainment on entry, are we all confident in assessing children's learning in maths? The data collected is only part of the picture; it doesn't stand alone but serves as another tool to be used within the context of all that is known about the children, provision and practitioners. There could be a danger of the individual characters, strengths, abilities and the motivations of young children to learn becoming devalued or lost, being reduced to a data set that solely reflects progress in the areas of learning, far removed from the real child. The individual circumstances and experiences of the child are not explicit in the data. Data raises questions, it may provide 'broad brushstrokes' as a useful tool – real depth of knowledge and understanding of progress can be found through robust consideration of the whole picture, everything we know about the children's learning within the setting and beyond.

Indeed some leaders and managers may note that the tracking data produced through the tracking systems does not reveal anything new; they were already aware of general trends that may emerge and progress made. It is another form of evidence. However, it may be useful as an extra source of evidence that is clear, 'easy to access' and understand

and therefore used to discuss progress with those who are not as informed or knowledgeable about the setting.

The collation and analysis of the data enables leaders and managers, who may not work directly with the children on a regular basis, to have a further insight into the learning and development of the children they are responsible for. In analysing the data, leaders and managers may be able to lead staff to plan more informed actions to ensure they can provide appropriate support for practice, practitioners and provision.

Trying tracking

Generally, when beginning to track progress, managers will collate data from the summative assessments made at regular intervals. Practitioners will make a progress review or summative assessment across all areas of learning and development and then also make a comparison (of 'attainment') to typical developmental norms for the children's age/stage. Developmental norms would be sourced from the setting's agreed child development guide to ensure consistent comparative data.

For example, a practitioner can use all their knowledge of a child gathered through observational assessment, to judge that at this point in time, a child is at a level that is just working within (or entering) the 30–50 months age/stage band as described in the Early Outcomes Guidance for Speaking. This isn't a checklist that is ticked off, but rather deciding on a 'best-fit' that most reliably describes the child's level of development at that point of assessment. Likewise, the practitioner would make 'best-fit' judgements across all areas of learning to compile comparative data for the child.

This comparative data will be passed to the manager and then collated in an electronic database or even a paper version. Over time the manager will build up a history of the child's development across the areas of learning, which will enable him/her to track and analyse progress made. The manager can then go on to compare groups of children to consider how they are progressing in relation to their starting points and developmental norms.

Managers can use the data to:

- Compare progress of groups – for example, girls compared with boys, children with additional needs and children without additional needs etc.
- Identify if there is an area of learning (or aspect of an area e.g. speaking) where a large proportion of children are working at a stage well below their chronological age and then plan for developments.
- Assess any apparent impact as a result of developments in practice – have more opportunities for and more creative and challenging outdoor provision made a difference to the progress of children in the prime areas?
- Monitor progress of all individual children.

Tracking traumas

A note of caution; moderation of judgements is essential. Unreliable assessments made by one practitioner may stand out as an obvious trend as all the data is compared. However, in small settings or settings with a majority of staff still developing their practice, unreliable judgements may be harder to identify.

The leaders and manager must ensure that assessments are reliable. At the beginning of this chapter we suggested that a sound knowledge of child development and a robust system for observation, assessment and planning must be in place; this cannot be over emphasised. Over reliance on analysis of an unmonitored data set could lead to complacency. If managers do not ensure reliability, the data generated is not robust, essentially of little value, and possibly even damaging as poor progress and provision may be masked and not acted upon. A time-consuming exercise could turn into a 'waste of time' exercise!

The moderation consideration

Moderation is a process that uses professional dialogue to agree judgements made. Currently there is a statutory obligation for local authorities to moderate judgements made in line with national exemplification materials for the Early Years Foundation Stage Profile, to ensure a sound national data set.

Managers and leaders can facilitate moderation between practitioners within their settings as well as moderating judgements themselves to ensure reliability. The process can be carried out in a number of ways to be decided by the manager and team.

For example:

- The manager may observe the setting in action and select a child of interest with whom to interact, play and to observe.
- Using evidence collated by the Key Person, the manager can reflect on observations, assessments and plans collected over time.
- Then in a professional dialogue with the Key Person the manager can facilitate a discussion around the child, his strengths, areas to develop and interests.
- Together the manager and practitioner should consider assessments made in the areas of learning.
- The practitioner can share why the judgements made are the 'best fit' for that child within that age stage band.
- Together they will agree if the evidence, anecdotal and recorded, suggests the assessment is reliable.

To summarise, settings may track progress to:

- Ensure every child is making progress in all areas over time.
- Ensure every child's needs are met regardless of their level of development.
- Reflect on quality of the provision in all areas.
- Look at the progress of groups of children, for example boys, girls, children with additional needs etc. Compare, analyse and take next steps to ensure all groups have equal opportunities, access and can make progress.
- Identify any anomalies and then explore and question why.
- Ensure all practitioners are making reliable assessments of their children.
- Identify strengths and areas of development in practice and provision.
- Inform planning and practice.
- Analyse on-going trends over time and forward plan as a result. This may include next steps such as staff training, supporting home learning, engaging with outside agencies or developing the learning environment.
- Enable parents and other stakeholders to celebrate children's progress made over time.

Ways to track progress:

Settings may track progress in a number of ways. Electronic monitoring tools such as Progress monitor or PRAMS may be in use. Many products are available to support managers and leaders. In schools, the same tracking systems may be used from the Reception year to year 6 in order to track and analyse progress over time.

Other settings may track progress using their own electronic systems they have devised.

Some settings may choose to use paper/hard copy methods to collate the data and then analyse their findings.

Settings may consider the needs of all stakeholders when deciding ways to track progress.

Tracking Top Tip – reliable assessments are essential!

Why is a reliance on numerical data unnecessary and potentially harmful in Early Years education?

This was first written in 2012 by Margaret Edgington for the newsletter of the National Campaign for Real Nursery Education and is reproduced with permission in edited and updated form.

I, along with many others, have become increasingly concerned about the increase in the number of schools and settings relying on numerical data when discussing children's progress. Indeed, it seems that some OFSTED inspectors are only interested in data and have been dismissing the carefully prepared portfolios showing children's learning journeys, progress reviews and learning priorities. It is my opinion that this development is not only unnecessary, but also leads to a misrepresentation of the excellent work of the best Early Years practitioners. Additionally, there seems to me to be a real danger that thinking about children in terms of data will distort practitioners' view of their individual characteristics.

I must make it clear that I am not against tracking children's progress. However, because each child is unique with their own prior experiences, interests, strengths, ways of learning and pattern of development, I believe that any meaningful tracking can only focus on the individual. I do not see how comparing data on groups of children is of any relevance at this stage in children's lives, since groups of children (e.g. EAL, boys, children from a particular ethnic or social group) are likely to be made up of individuals with diverse needs and characteristics and are likely to be too small for any meaningful comparisons to be made. For this reason, more than one strategy would be required to support development. Additionally, children's pace of development varies greatly at this stage in their lives. This is perfectly normal and often a few months more life experience makes all the difference. Unless practitioners focus on each child carefully as an individual, there is a real danger that some children will be seen as 'failing' or 'behind' and given some kind of intervention programme when, in fact, they simply need to be given more time or experience.

The UK has a long tradition (led by maintained nursery schools) of observation based assessment, which includes regular progress reviews (usually undertaken by the whole team involved with the child) when interests, strengths and new developments are noted and any learning priorities are identified and planned for. Because of the relatively small scale of Early Years' settings, senior staff tend to know the children and families very well. They also monitor and evaluate all aspects of their provision systematically and thoroughly and should therefore be aware of any strengths and weaknesses in provision and any barriers to children's learning. Effective senior staff also regularly review records of achievement, notice any gaps or weaknesses and then discuss with staff whether these are because opportunities are not being provided for children, or because staff lack confidence in recognising these aspects of development.

It is difficult to see what looking at crude data drawn up from nationally prescribed, and politically influenced, levels of development can add to this deep knowledge. What it can do is lead to practitioners reducing children to ability levels or numbers and ultimately narrowing their view of them. This is surely not why anyone started to work with very young children. Some head teachers and managers admit they produce data simply for OFSTED inspection and this worries me greatly. Others say they find data useful? This is also worrying, as it implies that leaders of Early Years' settings have lost confidence in their expertise in knowing individual children. Do we really want to sell ourselves short and mask our excellent and unique work which truly does put the unique child at the centre of our thinking and practice?

OFSTED now makes it clear, in Subsidiary Guidance provided for inspectors of schools and Early Years settings, that the age bands in Development Matters and the Early Learning Outcomes 2014 are non-statutory guidance and that inspectors should be judging the setting's own approach to assessment and their knowledge of the children. If inspectors continue to demand data based on these non-statutory materials, please tell them politely that these are Non-Statutory Guidance and you are not required to use them in this way. Explain your approach to personalised assessment and insist that inspectors look at your carefully completed records/portfolios and examine progress reviews. Tell them how you monitor and evaluate your practice to ensure that the provision meets the needs of all children, and give examples of how any weaknesses are quickly spotted and addressed. Above all, promote the excellence of Early Years' practice in understanding and meeting the needs of each individual child.

Appendices: some useful sheets

A framework for explaining a setting's approach

Observation and assessment at ……… (*insert name of setting*)

At ………… setting all adults are encouraged to:

Make observations as they work with the children – they notice children's significant achievements/new developments as they work with them – these are recorded quickly on Post-it notes/sticky labels, with a note of the EYFS area of learning and development they relate to and stuck in date order into the child's Learning Journal/development record. Photos and pieces of mark-making that show significant developments are also collected and a note is made to show what was significant. Staff use the information they gain from these observations to adapt weekly and daily planning, so that it is responsive to the children's needs and interests.

Parents are encouraged to contribute photos and/or their observations of their child's achievements and experiences at home.

Make focused or planned observations of each unique child – each week …. (*insert number*) children are chosen for all staff members in the team to focus on. These observations are usually made when children are initiating their own play, so that adults can learn about each child as a unique individual. The observer analyses their observation and records an assessment of the significant development and learning it shows for the child – the assessment statements are linked to the EYFS areas of Learning and Development, but adults are encouraged to use their own words to describe the child's unique achievements. These children are discussed by the team at the end of the week and their learning priorities/next steps are identified – when identifying next steps adults may refer to the Development Matters Statements in the EYFS Practice Guidance or to the Early Learning Outcomes or to child development texts, but often use their own words to write a clear, jargon free next step for a child. Relevant experiences that would help each child achieve their next steps are identified and each Key Person ensures that these experiences feature in the planning over the next few weeks. Parents are involved in this and are encouraged to support their child at home.

Each Key Person reviews the Learning Journals for their group and lets other team members know if there are any particular strengths or gaps. Senior leaders also regularly look at a sample of Learning Journals and feedback to the relevant staff.

Progress Reviews are carried out every ………… (e.g. term, half term, 3 months). Using practitioners' and parents' knowledge of the child and evidence in the child's Learning Journal as well as the setting's agreed child development guide, a Progress review sheet is completed and learning priorities set. This is used as a transition record when children move between rooms or settings.

The role of the practitioner who is supporting and extending child-initiated activity (sometimes called the 'float' role)

General supervisory roles

- help children with their personal needs (e.g. toileting, putting coats on etc.);
- manage crises – re-stock resources;
- be aware of snack bar and support where necessary;
- be aware of safety but encourage risk-taking;
- help children access resources;
- notice children who need help to get involved (who might be on the edges, looking a bit lost);
- notice where children are in free-flow settings and make sure staffing is appropriate (i.e. if a majority of children have gone outside, the 'float' should follow).

Their role in supporting and extending child-initiated learning (NB support and extension should be brief) – always observe first and never take over from the child

- enhancing the area/experience with additional resources;
- role modelling:
  - how to use and care for equipment
  - appropriate behaviour
  - language
  - roles in play (e.g. modelling the role of the doctor or patient in hospital role play for a few minutes)
- giving information/explaining;
- asking open-ended questions to promote thinking ('What do you think will happen if'? 'How do you think you could?');
- encouraging problem solving ('What else could you use/try?');
- making suggestions ('Have you thought about', 'What about trying');
- praising giving clear feedback ('I really liked the way you worked with S to....');
- mediating – helping children to share, work together and resolve conflict.

Some interactive strategies

STRATEGY	WHEN TO USE
Adding to the provision	In response to observation or to arouse curiosity
Acting as a role model	To introduce new skills, language or ideas; to help children see the role of skills such as reading and writing
Demonstrating skills or sharing knowledge	To introduce equipment that has to be used in a particular way (e.g. scissors); to support a child who wants/needs a skill or some knowledge
Acknowledging and articulating a child's interests, actions or feelings (running commentary)	To show the child she/he is noticed/valued; to model language to help the child express him/herself
Sharing own experiences in conversational style	To help children make connections between home and nursery or pre-school; to engage children with story telling
Scaffolding individual children	To enable the child to take the next step or to get involved with others
Asking open-ended questions – posing problems	To find out what children know and to challenge and extend their thinking and language

Observation, assessment and planning

Some frequently asked questions

Addressed by Margaret Edgington, Independent Early Years Consultant

How many observations do I need per child?

The only sensible answer to this question is that we need to be able to show that we know each child really well as a unique individual. Many observations (which must always describe factually what the child does, and should include accurate examples of what the child has said) can be remembered without recording and can be shared verbally. It is not possible to hold everything in our minds though and, for this reason, it is essential to develop a Learning Journal for each child, which includes quick notes, longer narrative observations, annotated photos and pieces of mark-making and which shows their progress over time. There is no set amount of evidence.

Do we have to match each observation to a point in *Development Matters*?

No. *Development Matters* is non-statutory guidance material and it makes it clear on nearly every page that it should not be used as a checklist. Current advice is that it can be used, when carrying out Progress reviews, to identify which age band is a 'best fit' with the child's current stage of development. Children do not have to have achieved every point in a band.

Does every observation need a next step?

No. Many observations simply tell us something significant about the child's development. It is often necessary to have a number of observations of a child to be able to identify what their next learning priority should be. Sometimes, an adult notices a child is struggling with something and gives immediate support – this involves observing, assessing, identifying a learning need and acting on that need without any recording. Many practitioners find it useful to identify a small number of children they will focus on each week and then, at the end of the week, they discuss what they have learnt about the children, identify one or two learning priorities for them and share these with parents.

Should each Key Person observe only their key children?

No. In most settings a team of practitioners works with all the children and it is very valuable to have these different perspectives on children's development and learning. It is also important that all adults know the children well, so they can work with them effectively. Children form different relationships, and often show different aspects of their development, with each adult. The Key Person needs these additional perspectives in order to get a broader view of their key children – this is important for every Key Person, but particularly important for less experienced practitioners.

Index

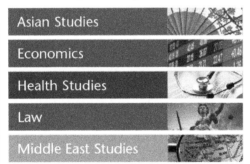
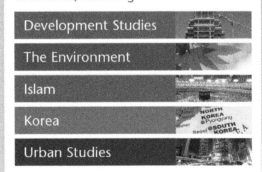